GW00457309

Conducting Business Analysis: An Optimized Approach

Stuart Shafran

Preface

There are already hundreds of books out there describing various aspects of business analysis, so why on earth would we need yet another one? Well, the simple answer is that maybe we don't. And yet, for someone new to business analysis there are always some crucial questions that need answering; where should I start? Which methodology should I follow? Which techniques are useful and which are not? How do you get from that initial request to do a piece of work, to the point where you have a complete understanding of the problem and some well documented information that points towards a useful solution?

Well, like anything in life, you basically have a choice. You can attend lots of courses to learn about business analysis. You can trawl through lots of books about business analysis. Each of these books and courses will help you to a certain degree, but they will also bog you down and confuse you as to the right or wrong way of doing things. You will find conflicting information about the best way to write a use case or a requirement or a user story. You will find that one writer recommends doing one thing while another recommends doing something completely different. So what approach should you use, and why?

The only way you will really improve your analysis skills is by doing. This book is all about the doing – it describes a particular approach to business analysis that can be used for any piece of work, no matter how large or small the project. I am describing an approach that is straightforward and very simple to implement. Once you know what you're doing and why you're doing it, the approach described is extremely fast and has proven to be successful on numerous projects.

So, going back to my original question – why do we need yet another book about business analysis? The answer is that this book will provide you with something a little different from all the other books out there. It will provide you with a particular approach that will give you the ability to perform business analysis in the most efficient way possible. It will also provide you with examples on how to think like an analyst, and this is absolutely crucial.

But the main difference between this book and most other books on business analysis is that this book concentrates on the performing of requirements *derivation* instead of requirements *gathering*. Now, what do I mean by that? Requirements gathering, often known as 'elicitation' is the process of obtaining and documenting requirements. Traditionally, a requirements engineer or an analyst will set up workshops, have brainstorming sessions and pro-actively concentrate on gathering the requirements needed to describe the solution to a problem. The approach described in this book however, concentrates on *deriving* requirements i.e. obtaining requirements indirectly from specific analysis techniques. You may still need workshops and brainstorming sessions but you will not be specifically asking for requirements in these sessions. You will however, be using some very specific analysis techniques in order to gain a good understanding of the problem area i.e. you will be building a firm 'knowledge base'.

There is a difference in approach and workflow between documenting a list of requirements via direct questioning and performing requirements derivation via techniques such as process and concept mapping. If you ask people directly for their requirements and you ask the right questions, you will probably obtain a fairly good picture of what is required. A picture that is maybe 80% complete. Now, regardless as to whether you are involved in an 'agile' development methodology or a 'waterfall' development methodology, there are going to be gaps; things that are overlooked. You are never going to obtain a complete picture without several months or even years of work. These omissions can cause problems and they can cost money.

However, if you establish a good knowledge base up front from which you can derive (and validate) requirements, you are far less likely to experience gaps and missed requirements. Not only that, but the process of establishing a good knowledge base via analysis is significantly faster. This is a 'rapid' and iterative approach to analysis and can be used alongside development methodologies such as 'waterfall' or the various flavours of 'agile'. The time spent moving from problem to solution will be significantly reduced.

So this book is all about an approach that is designed to help you as a business analyst establish a strong knowledge base that can be used to describe both the original problem as well as the future solution. The book describes a set of very useful and specific techniques that you can use for business analysis and explains how and when to use each technique. And it explains how you can obtain a set of clearly written, unambiguous and testable requirements quickly and efficiently, via analysis rather than direct questioning.

This book has been created for the person who knows nothing about business analysis, the complete beginner, but it's also a book for the experienced analyst who may want to optimize his or her techniques. In practical terms this book represents a distillation of over 14 years personal experience as a business analyst, including knowledge gained from numerous books and courses as well as hands-on practical experience. Hopefully the reader will gain something useful from the reading!

Acknowledgements

I would like to thank Cuiming Zheng and Jacqueline White, (both business analysts themselves), for helping to review this book and for providing me with very useful feedback.

I would also like to thank the following in particular for all their help, advice and encouragement during the writing of this book:

Louisa Noffke

Dominic Pennington

Lizzie Scuffell

Daniel Perrin

Thanks also to Darryl Kempster for being the cover model for this book.

I would also like to thank my two cats, Honey and Belle, for creating havoc every time I sat down to write; their distraction techniques succeeded in forcing me to revisit the text multiple times.

Last but not least, I would like to thank my wife Jodi for her continuous support and for acting as a sounding board for some of my more crazy ideas, even though she didn't have the faintest idea what I was talking about!

Contents

Chapter 1 - Business Analysis

What is business analysis?

I am only going to give a very brief summary on this, as there are many books already out there which describe what business analysis is in great detail. If you want to know how business analysis originated and what a business analyst does then I would refer you to a book called 'Business Analysis' by Debra Paul and Donald Yeates. This book is published by the BCS (British computer Society). Another good source of material for learning about business analysis is the BABOK - A guide to the Business Analysis Body of Knowledge published by the International Institute of Business Analysis. In fact I'm going to quote directly from this guide in order to summarize in one paragraph what business analysis is:

'Business analysis is the set of tasks and techniques used to work as a liaison among stakeholders in order to understand the structure, policies, and operations of an organization, and to recommend solutions that enable the organization to achieve its goals'.

There, a nice definition straight from the BABOK, the business analyst's bible so to speak. The person who liaises among these stakeholders and uses the set of task and techniques to gain an understanding of the organization is of course, the Business Analyst. Now, I'm not going to waste your time and mine by repeating what has already been written; suffice it to say that my understanding of what a business analyst does can be summarized as follows:

Someone or numerous someone's have a problem. They need to solve this problem. They call on someone with skill in the art of problem solving to take a look at their problem and help them work out a solution to the problem. Now, if the problem is with a leaky toilet, you would probably contact a plumber. If the electrics have blown, you contact an electrician. So in what circumstances would you need to contact a business analyst? Well, the clue is in the definition above. An organization needs to achieve certain goals. Obviously, this organization must have some sort of problem with achieving its goals; otherwise there would be no need for the skills of a business analyst. However, unlike the case of a leaky toilet or dodgy electrics, the problem is not something that can be addressed by fixing a physical object. The problems that require business analysis skills are not physical problems; they are metaphysical problems, i.e. these are issues that require clarification of fundamental notions of understanding within a particular domain.

Business analysis comprises three parts:
- an input
- an analysis of that input
- an output

The input consists of information about the problem or issue that you have been assigned to tackle. If the information you obtain is clearly understandable and provides a comprehensive knowledge base, you (and any other interested parties) will be able to make good use of it. This input needs to be properly structured in order to make it comprehensible and suitable for analysis.

The analysis of the input is the most important part of the business analyst's job. This is what differentiates a good business analyst from a poor one. There are many computer programs that can analyze input and create output automatically, but currently there is no automated way of conducting proper business analysis by using a computer based tool. The conducting of business analysis is a flexible process i.e. the analyst has to be able to adapt to circumstances that can quickly change. The analysis can involve various techniques, several iterations and a lot of human interaction.

The third part is the output and this also needs to be structured correctly to be of use. The output a business analyst creates has to contain the information necessary and in sufficient detail for the creation of a solution. There are various tools you can use to document input and to document output, but to conduct proper business analysis as opposed to just creating documentation, you will need to use the human brain. You have to be able to understand the input. You have to be able to analyze that input properly in order to create an output and the output has to be useful, understandable and correct.

Business analysis is all about gaining a good metaphysical understanding of the way things work within a specific space. The concepts, the properties of those concepts, cause and effect, the what and the why… it's about process, it's about logic, it's about using the knowledge and understanding of the domain to drive forward to a solution to the problem. This also gives a small clue as to who is likely to make a good business analyst. The two main skills a good business analyst needs are the ability to think logically and the ability to listen. A business analyst also needs to be able to challenge, to ask the question 'why?' and to think creatively.

Now, most of the time a business analyst is recruited to address an issue with system software or to improve a process involving software, but there is no reason why a business analyst should be restricted to working with software. In theory, you can use business analysis to address any metaphysical problem… from something heavily philosophical such as 'what do we mean by quality?' to something as mundane as 'what phone should I buy'? Although I will be touching on a couple of non-software related problems as examples, in this book I'm going to mostly concentrate on problems relating to software, because this is what the majority of business analysts are employed to tackle.

The three rules of business analysis

You're probably not going to find these rules described as such in any other book, but these are the fundamental rules that every business analyst needs to follow, and I'm going to explain exactly why.

The three rules of business analysis are:

1. Process is everything!
2. Beware of assumptions!
3. Requirements before solution!

There is actually a very important fourth rule as well:

Keep things simple!

But this rule can be applied to a lot of things outside business analysis including the whole of life, so I'll stick to the first three rules for now and touch fairly continuously on the generic fourth rule as we work through the examples described in this book.

So, **rule number one** – Process is everything. Why is process everything? What do I mean by this?

First of all, what do we mean by a 'process'? Here I'm going to refer you to an excellent book called 'workflow modeling' by Alec Sharp. Alec goes into a lot of detail describing exactly what a process is. Essentially, a process is a sequence of inter-related steps or activities that begin with a triggering event and end with a result or outcome. A single process describes the series of steps relating to one particular object or task. So for example, cutting a tree down would be one process as it relates to a single task and a single object (the tree). Making a telephone call would be a single (and completely separate) process. These two processes may be related e.g. after you've cut a tree down you might go and phone a friend to tell them that you've just cut a tree down, but essentially these are separate processes. And that's about as far as I'm going to go for now with describing what a process is, because Alec Sharp has already described everything you need to know about process and workflow modeling in the above mentioned book. There will be lots of references to process later, but for now if you require more in depth information then go buy Alec's book!

Basically, everything we do in life is based around process. When you get up in the morning, when you go to bed at night, when you cook food or drive to work you are performing a particular process, you are following a particular sequence of steps one after the other until you finish with one process and begin another. You want to watch a program on television? This is the process:

1. Switch on TV
2. Find program to watch
3. Watch the program

There are numerous points in the process where decisions are made and the process can diverge off into a different series of steps or even a different process entirely. There are even processes that you will perform unconsciously i.e. you are not even aware that you are following a particular process when you go through the steps. Essentially, we can look on life as conducting a series of processes, triggered by different events and resulting in various outcomes that lead on to further processes…

And this is the reason why process is everything. Whenever someone wants to do something, that someone will carry out a particular process to achieve a goal. In the world of organizations and software related activities, people are running through a series of activities, one step after another, to achieve an objective. You want to print a report? There's a particular process for doing that. You want to record some data in a software system? Or find the answer to a particular question? You have to follow a process. The entire approach described in this book is all based on process… gaining an understanding of what processes are currently used and what processes are needed in the future. This gives clarity on where we are today and where we want to be in the future. It's a fundamental concept and the heart of the entire approach – process is everything! Understand the process and why the process is being carried out and what the problems are with an existing process and you're already more than halfway there!

Rule number two – Beware of assumptions. As a business analyst, a large part of your job is going to be communicating with stakeholders – people who have a particular interest and/or expert knowledge in the subject or domain that you've been assigned to work on. You will need to gain a good understanding of what the users (the people who will be using the solution) currently do and what they want to do in the future. Often, a user may assume that you have more knowledge about the domain than you actually have. The user may tell you things without providing a complete set of information, leading you to make erroneous assumptions. An example - if someone says to you that they drive to work, you might assume that they are driving a car. It's a logical assumption, most people drive to work every day in a car. However, that person may be driving a lorry. He (or she) may be driving a tractor. A statement taken out of context (we don't know what the drivers' job is) leads us to an automatic assumption that the driver is driving a car.

Making assumptions with regards software is very common. Are you going to assume that the problematic software currently being used now is still going to be used in the future? That the current operating system will still be in use three years from now? That the volume of data being recorded into the database will not suddenly undergo a massive increase due to a change in process? Beware of assumptions… never take anything at face value. Never assume that you've covered everything there is to cover with the users… there is always some little detail missing. Ask lots of questions to try to cover every eventuality you can think of. You will never cover them all but it's definitely worth trying; you never know what will suddenly appear!

Whenever an assumption appears, make sure that you document it as an assumption; never overlook it. You need to state the assumptions clearly and up front; you need to discuss assumptions with the stakeholders to ensure that these assumptions are correct. By doing this you are reducing (but certainly not eliminating) the chances of some unforeseen circumstance happening that will cause problems further down the line.

Lastly, **rule number three**. Requirements before solution. This does seem like such an obvious rule – how can you get to a solution without knowing what the requirements are for that solution? Quite easily, actually. It's often the case that the users think they know exactly what the problem is, what their requirements are and what the solution needs to be. Back to rule number 2 – beware of assumptions… never assume that your users know what their problems are or what the requirements are. The chances are, they may well be wrong. Users often base their requirements on existing tools that they're using. Or alternatively, they often base their requirements on what they think should be the solution, based again on current usage of tools. In these cases they are not thinking in terms of *what* they do… the process… they are thinking in terms of *how* they do it, based on the tools they currently have available.

Or maybe it's the Project Manager or Architect driving the push towards a quick solution. Again, this is caused by basing a decision on assumptions that may or may not be correct. Or it could be caused by a time factor driving the need to complete a project quickly. Or by the development process itself – a seemingly 'agile' process that involves defining all of the requirements on the fly as the solution is being developed without any real understanding of the process or the underlying problem. This latter situation is not really acceptable. Agile development methodologies can be very successful and the approach discussed in this book does relate to a very agile and iterative way of working. However, using an agile development methodology is not an excuse for failing to define a proper 'To Be' process and a set of problem statements and business requirements up front. As we shall see when we come to the approach itself, it's all about the level of detail that needs to be defined up front. A 'waterfall' approach involves defining a set of requirements in great detail up front and getting these requirements signed off by the users before any development work can proceed. An agile or iterative approach involves obtaining a good knowledge base up front that is of sufficient detail to enable a developer to begin work. The rest of the detail can be defined during the development phase.

Selecting a solution before you have a clear idea of what the real problems and business requirements are can be very dangerous and could potentially lead to a failed project and a lot of wasted money. The answer is to stick to rule three – don't begin work on the solution until you know what the requirements are. It will save a lot of pain in the long run.

Chapter 2 – The Approach

The approach described in this book is focused primarily on the following two points:

1. You reuse as much information as you can. It can be very daunting when you first begin work on a new project, especially if that project is within a domain area that you are not particularly familiar with. You do have one major advantage though, that you **must** exploit. At least ninety nine percent of the time, no matter what industry you are working in, someone somewhere has done something very similar. Take a look at what other people have done within your domain area, both within and outside your company. Find requirements that other people have written which might be relevant. Use the internet and take a look at the other systems and solutions that are already available on the market. You do not have to reinvent the wheel! I guarantee that there will be something useful out there that you can reuse; you just have to do the research.

2. You build a firm knowledge base from which you can derive requirements. This knowledge base is a comprehensive, mostly pictorial representation of the problem area. You create this knowledge base by reusing as much information as you can, but also by concentrating on three things in particular, which I am referring to in this book as 'principals' for want of a better word. You will need to combine your reuse of relevant material with the three principals to build your knowledge base in order for you to derive the requirements.

The Three Principals

The idea here is that by focusing on three key principals when conducting your analysis work, everything else will fall pretty much into place. There is one caveat… the three principals are time based i.e. you will need to obtain knowledge of these three principals within the context of what is currently happening and what needs to happen in the future.

So what am I actually talking about here? What exactly are these three 'principals'?

Well, the first one is fairly obvious if you've just read chapter one about the three rules… it's process. Rule number one - process is everything – process is the first of the three principals you need to be concerned about as an analyst. The second is concepts, or 'things'. You really need to have a good understanding about the things that are relevant to whatever you're dealing with and a clear definition of what these things actually are. Finally, the third principal that you need to gain knowledge about is not 'requirements' as many might think… it's actually 'functionality' i.e. the capability to do something with or to a 'thing'.

Now if you've read some books about business analysis and been on training courses, this might actually sound counter to what many analysts are currently doing… surely business analysis is all about eliciting (gathering) and documenting the requirements? Yes, defining the requirements is one of the ultimate aims, but where this approach differs from other approaches is that instead of focusing on requirements gathering, you will be concentrating on defining the processes, concepts and functionalities first and deriving the requirements from workflows based on these three principals. To explain, we need to understand exactly what we mean by the term 'requirement'.

A requirement is a **need** to do something with or to a 'thing'. This is subtly different from a functionality, which is the *ability* (rather than the need) to do something with or to a 'thing'. *'I need to record an identifier for a project'* is a clearly written requirement. The requirement consists of two parts… a 'doing' part and a part describing the 'thing' or 'things' that are involved. The doing part can be regarded as process… the act of recording or documenting something is a process step. The identifier and the project are 'things'. The identifier belongs to the project, so 'identifier' is an attribute of a project. The project itself can be regarded as a 'concept' (a concept is a type of object… something of substance or maybe an abstract idea). So a requirement actually has two components – a process component and a concept component. By understanding the relationship between process and concepts you can derive requirements.

A 'functionality' is the ability to do something with or to a 'thing'. I'm calling it functionality here because in terms of a system, the ability to do something is a piece of functionality. It can also be regarded as a 'business' level requirement or an objective, because it provides the purpose for the more detailed functional requirements. An example functionality might be 'the ability to create a project'.

What you have here is an inter-related triangle:

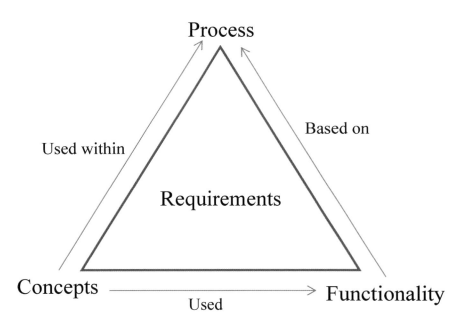

I am not going to go into any more detail about process, concepts, functionalities or requirements here; you will need to read the rest of the book to find out how this works! Even if this doesn't make sense to you now, bear with me and things should start coming together as you progress through the chapters. Suffice to say, this entire approach is centered on gaining knowledge of these three principals – process (the doing), concepts (the things) and functionalities (the capability), as quickly and efficiently as possible. Once you have these three principals properly defined for your problem area, you will have created a firm knowledge base. As you progress through the approach you will be expanding that knowledge base to include other useful things such as problems, scope, constraints (including business and system rules) and of course, requirements.

The three phase approach

I said that gaining knowledge of the above three principals is based within the context of time. In relation to the approach, this actually translates into a three phase approach, starting with the present and working towards the future via a 'transition' phase. The first phase is to gain a good understanding about what is currently happening now. The second phase is to start working out what is needed for the future, a sort of 'transition' phase. The third phase is delving into more detail about the future. I will be going into more detail on this in just a minute. First, let's take a look at the following diagram, where I'll try to explain what I mean by this approach:

Fig. 1 – A Process diagram describing the three phase approach:

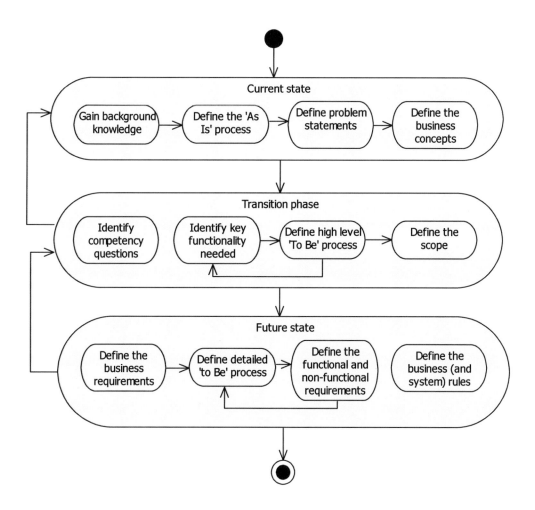

This diagram represents a simplistic overview of the whole approach that we will be discussing in the following chapters. Fig. 1 is a very basic process diagram that shows a start point at the top and an end point at the bottom (the red circles). The start point represents the beginning of the process, the point where you have just been told that you're working on a new piece of work. The end point represents the point in time when you should have sufficient information about what needs to be done for a solution to be developed. How long it takes to get from the start point to the end point is very much dependent on how big and complicated the piece of work is, how many users you need to deal with and how quickly you can reach a consensus on what the 'To Be' process is going to look like. Getting from start to end can take anything from a few days to a few weeks; possibly even a few months for a very large piece of work.

Note that the end point represents the point in time when you have a comprehensive set of information available in order to start building a solution. Development work can actually begin sooner i.e. during the future state phase, dependent on the type of project you are working on and whether or not you are using an 'agile' or 'iterative' development methodology. I will return to this topic later... for now I'll just reiterate that this is a business analysis approach, not a development approach and the objective is to obtain the knowledge necessary for an informed decision to be made regarding a solution to a particular problem. You may well be in a position to make an informed decision about the solution without having to work through each and every step in the process. However, your job as a business analyst will probably require your involvement during the development of the solution and you will probably need to revisit and flesh out the requirements in an iterative manner. We will discuss this further in the chapter on requirements.

In between the start and the end points are three large boxes containing several smaller boxes, with the arrows showing the order of sequence. The large boxes represent the three phases that you will progress through as you follow the approach. The smaller boxes represent process steps that need to be carried out for each phase.

Over the next few chapters we will be examining in detail how to carry out each of the processes described. For now though, let us quickly run through and summarize the approach as described in the diagram in fig. 1.

The approach can be broken down into three phases:

- A 'current state' phase, where the activities that you carry out are done specifically to allow you to gain sufficient knowledge to provide a good understanding of what is currently going on with regards to whatever issue you have been assigned to work on.
- A 'transition' phase, where you are carrying out activities specifically to work towards gaining a good understanding of the 'future state'. It is very hard to jump from an understanding of the current state to an understanding of the future state without going through any transitional activities. Notice the arrow pointing back from the transition phase to the current state – you may need to revisit some of the artifacts you have defined for the current state
- A 'future state' phase, where the activities you carry out are done specifically to define what the future state is going to look like. At this point you may already be in a position to begin

work on the solution. Again, there is an arrow pointing backwards from the future state to the transition phase, indicating that you may need to revisit artifacts that you have defined in the transition phase as more information becomes available.

This phased approach is pretty straightforward – you have to gain some understanding of the current state of whatever you are working on, and then work out what the future state (the solution) is going to look like. The devil is in the detail though, and the detail is defined by the activities within these phases.

The Current Phase

Let's start with the current phase. The process begins with gaining some background knowledge to the issue(s) before you can progress. Without at least some rudimentary knowledge of what the issue involves and what the objective is, how can you work out what the problems are? Even with some knowledge of the background, it may still be difficult to determine what the real problems are so you will need to understand what it is your users are currently doing. The best way to do this is to map out the 'As Is' process - the current way of working for the users. As you work through defining what your users are currently doing, the problems they are facing become far more apparent. You may still need to perform some 'root cause analysis' to get to the 'real' problems, but with a good understanding of both the 'As Is' process and the background, you should have a much clearer idea about the problems that need to be addressed.

You should also be noticing two other things as you define the 'As Is' process with the users - terminology and concepts. Certain terms will be used by the users that may or may not be familiar to you. These will need to be noted down and described properly in a glossary of terms. At the same time, some of these terms may well be key concepts that can be mapped onto a diagram to show the relationship between them. We will come on to this in a later chapter…

Up to this point, we have been concentrating solely on trying to understand the current situation; we have not ventured into the realms of the future, although it is highly likely that some discussion of future requirements may have popped up during the process described above. As soon as all the above artifacts have been described and documented though, you should be in a good position to begin work on describing what needs to be done in the future to tackle the problems and work towards a relevant solution.

The Transitional Phase

So the next phase of work is the transitional phase. This is the point where you begin transitioning your users from thinking about the current situation to thinking about the future. I cannot emphasize enough how important this phase is… both you and your users will have great difficulty jumping straight from the 'as is' to the 'to be' without some clear thought about how you are going to get there. Think of it as a type of journey… you are accompanying your users on a journey of exploration to map out what the future needs to look like. I have seen far too many projects where this phase has been totally skipped over, where the jump straight to requirements has resulted in missed requirements, requirements that have not been thought through properly or even requirements that are totally wrong.

The first activity in this phase (identify competency questions) isn't connected to the other activities in terms of process flow. 'Competency' questions (I'll explain what these are properly in a later chapter) are used to help define concepts and search criteria. Competency questions are particularly useful for projects involving data, especially data integration and / or querying and reporting. The use of competency questions can also be very beneficial for projects focusing on new ideas. You can use the competency question technique at any point within the first two phases of the approach.

If your project does not involve the need to work with data then you probably don't need to worry about competency questions too much. You do however need to worry about the key functionality that will be needed! For this approach, 'functionalities' can be more or less equated to business use cases. A use case is a sequence of actions that a user (or actor) performs to achieve a particular goal. A 'functionality' can also be regarded in these terms if you think of it as something that is required by a user in order to achieve a particular goal. By defining which business use cases (functionalities) are going to be required you are one step closer to working out what it is your users want to do.

This is where the 'To Be' process comes in. For many projects, defining what the users want to do in the future can be a challenge, but we will discuss how to address this challenge properly later in this book. You will notice an arrow pointing back from the 'To Be' process to the 'define key functionalities' process… this is because as you define the 'To Be' process you will probably need to revisit the business use cases as well. You will be asking the questions: has anything changed? Is all this functionality still required? Is there any additional functionality that is required in the future, based on the 'To Be' process? At this point we are nearly ready to move to the future state phase and start defining requirements.

Before we start moving into actual requirements though and delving into the detail, we need to take a look at the scope. The scope is very important. Everything that follows in terms of solution, including the extent of the work needed and the cost of that work is going to depend on what is being defined within the scope. Also important is what is defined as being out of scope, because no work should be carried out on anything that is deemed 'out of scope'. If you are working on things that are out of scope then you are effectively wasting your time.

The Future Phase

Moving on then, all the requirements and business rules definition can be considered to be 'future state' work. It should be possible to derive the high level business requirements from the business use cases. The business use cases that are deemed to be within scope can now be broken down into more detail by describing each piece of functionality in terms of the workflow that a user would envisage following in the future. The functional requirements, non-functional requirements and business rules also need to be defined during this phase. This is where all those individual pieces of the puzzle come together. The business concepts will help form some of the business rules, the information captured in the 'To Be' workflow diagrams for each business use case will become the basis for the functional requirements, and the non-functional requirements will need to be obtained using a pre-defined check list for non-functional requirements combined with careful questioning of the users.

Whether you document the functional requirements using detailed use cases, user stories or single sentence requirement statements is completely up to you. The choice may be based on the type of problem you are working on and whether or not you are following some form of 'agile' development methodology. However I will be recommending what I think is a useful and straightforward approach to requirements documentation and I will also be discussing the usefulness (or not) of creating requirements matrices linking one requirement to another.

Using the approach to address specific problems

Although the approach as described looks to be a very linear approach with lots of analytical activities to be carried out, this is actually not the case. When you follow this approach you will quickly realize that it is a very iterative, logical and efficient way of working. How much work you as an analyst need to do depends heavily on what you are working on – the type of problem you are tackling and the size of the problem. Let's take a quick look at some of the different types of problem you may be assigned to work on and see how the approach fits. We will number each activity within the approach and make a rough determination of which activities are relevant to which type of problem (this can be a little subjective though and depends heavily on the extent of the problem!):

Fig. 2 – A list of the analytical activities within the approach

Analytical Activity	Number
Gain background knowledge	1
Define the 'As Is' process	2
Define problem statements	3
Define the business concepts	4
Identify competency questions	5
Identify key functionality needed	6
Define high level 'To Be' process	7
Define the scope	8
Define the business requirements	9
Define detailed 'to Be' process (workflows)	10
Define the functional and non-functional requirements	11
Define the business (and system) rules	12

Fig. 3 - A list of some potential problem types

Type of problem	Minimum analytical activities recommended	Optional activities (depends on extent of problem)
Process improvement	1, 2, 3, 4, 6, 7, 8, 9, 10	5, 11, 12
Idea investigation	1, 3, 4, 5, 6, 7, 8, 9	2, 10, 11, 12
Transformation e.g. changes to an organization	1, 2, 3, 4, 6, 7, 8, 9	5, 10, 11, 12
Technology introduction	1, 2, 3, 4, 5, 6, 7, 8, 9	10, 11, 12
Security change	1, 2, 3, 4, 6, 7, 8, 9, 10	5, 11, 12
Proof of concept / prototype / pilot	1, 2, 3, 4, 6, 7, 8, 9	5, 10, 11, 12
Collaboration with another organization / company	1, 2, 3, 4, 6, 7, 8, 9	5, 10, 11, 12
Vendor assessment	1, 2, 3, 4, 6, 7, 8, 9	5, 10, 11, 12
Software / hardware purchase	1, 2, 3, 4, 6, 7, 8, 9, 10	5, 11, 12
Training and education	1, 2, 3, 6, 7, 8, 9	4, 5, 10, 11, 12
Bug fix (one or more)	1, 3, 8, 11	2, 4, 5, 6, 7, 9, 10, 12
Enhancement(s) / upgrade	1, 2, 3, 4, 6, 7, 8, 9, 10, 11, 12	5
Configuration	1, 2, 3, 4, 5, 6, 7, 8, 9, 10, 11, 12	
New build	1, 2, 3, 4, 5, 6, 7, 8, 9, 10, 11, 12	
Replacement	1, 2, 3, 4, 5, 6, 7, 8, 9, 10, 11, 12	
Disposal	1, 2, 3, 7, 8, 9	4, 5, 6, 10, 11, 12
Migration (e.g. data from one data source to another)	1, 2, 3, 4, 5, 6, 7, 8, 9	10, 11, 12
Integration (e.g. integrating data from multiple data sources)	1, 2, 3, 4, 5, 6, 7, 8, 9, 10, 11, 12	
Query and Reporting	1, 2, 3, 4, 5, 6, 7, 8, 9, 10, 11, 12	
Interface development	1, 2, 3, 4, 6, 7, 8, 9, 10, 11	5, 12

The above is by no means a comprehensive list!

Looking at the table in fig. 3 you will notice a couple of interesting points:

- An analyst's job is not just about documenting requirements. For some of these problems you may not even need to define detailed functional and non-functional requirements. A defined process, defined concepts and a set of agreed functionalities that can be easily translated into high level business requirements may be sufficient.

- Apart from a simple bug fix, no matter what type of problem you are working on, you really need to have a good understanding of the process, the concepts / terminology involved, and the functionality required. You also need to have defined the background and problem statements, but without one or more of the three principals on which the whole approach is based - process, concepts and functionality, you are not going to get very far. If you do nothing else, make sure that you concentrate first on gaining a good understanding of the background, 'as is' process and problem, and secondly on the concepts and functionality required.

So in summary, we are talking about conducting a phased approach to business analysis that consists of several activities based around gaining a good understanding of process, concepts and functionality. The activities are carried out in an iterative manner, where each step in the process may involve some backtracking to further clarify and refine information gathered from previous steps. We are talking about an approach that leads us to the point where we have gained a good understanding of the future state, sufficient to begin work on a solution.

Chapter 3 – Context and Background

The lost phone problem

Let's face it; the only way you are really going to become adept at conducting business analysis is by *doing* business analysis… you have to gain experience to become proficient; you have to learn to think like a business analyst. So how does a business analyst think? Well, for one, a business analyst needs to think very logically. A business analyst needs to be able to understand and interpret the information that is being provided by the users. A business analyst needs to be able to listen, absorb, interpret and make an accurate assessment in order to provide benefit to those users. The only way an analyst can properly do this is if the analyst is in a good position to do so. That is what this chapter is all about; setting the context, understanding the background to the issue, making sure that you as an analyst are in a good position to be able to help the users. It all begins with the background…

Joe Bloggs: "I can't believe it! I've lost my mobile phone! Lost all my contacts! It couldn't have happened at a worse time… phones are expensive and I have no money to buy as new one! It's a disaster!"

You: "Don't worry Joe; I think I can help you"

Joe Bloggs: "You can? You'll do that for me? Buy me a new phone?"

You: "Well no, not exactly. But I can help you choose a new phone to buy that won't cost you much money"

Joe Bloggs: "That's better than nothing. Ok, help me buy a new phone that can do everything I want it to do and won't cost me much money. You can do that?"

You: "I'll certainly try."

Joe Bloggs has lost his phone. He needs a new one. He doesn't have much money. He wants to do stuff with his phone but we don't know what stuff. We don't know what his budget is; just that he doesn't have much money. We don't even know why he wants a mobile phone; does he even really need one? We don't know much at all in fact… let's rectify that.

We need to ask Joe a series of questions to establish the background and context to his problem. The more we ask him, the more we'll learn. Some of the information Joe will tell us will be irrelevant to his problem, and some of it will be very relevant. At this stage, any information we can get out of him will be useful. Let's start by asking him the following, in no particular order:

1. Where did you lose your phone?
2. Was it an expensive phone?
3. Is the loss of the phone covered by insurance?
4. What type of phone was it?
5. Were you using the phone for business or for private use, or both?

6. If you had a new phone, what would you want to use it for in the future?
7. Was it just you using the phone or was it a shared phone?
8. Will it just be you using the phone in the future?
9. How often did you use your phone?
10. Would you use a new phone more often or less often in the future?
11. How much are you willing to spend on a new phone?
12. What sort of things were you doing with the phone apart from communicating e.g. taking photos? Playing games?
13. Do you really need a phone that can do all these things?
14. Why do you need to carry a phone around with you?

We can easily add a lot more questions to this list, but as a quick example this will do fine for now. You'll notice that some of these questions appear to be a little unnecessary... what does it matter where he lost the phone? Why ask him if it's a shared phone – most phones are purchased for use by a single individual. Isn't it obvious why he wants to carry a phone around with him? Be careful here; it's very easy to make assumptions because you are familiar in some way with part of the context. Remember rule number 2 – Beware of assumptions!

If Joe Bloggs lost his phone in the living room of his house, maybe he can find it again. If this is the case he no longer has a problem. If he dropped it off the edge of a cliff and it shattered on the way down then he has a problem, so this question is very relevant. Maybe Joe Bloggs shares his phone with his wife? It's possible. Does Joe Bloggs even have a wife? It's another question that provides information and it may or may not be relevant. Maybe he does have a wife and his wife sometimes uses the phone as well. Or his children...

The question asking *why* he needs a mobile phone is probably the most important question. It's also the most controversial, because unless the question is phrased properly it can sound like a challenge and that is definitely not the intention. Asking the question 'why' makes the user think... why does he actually need a mobile phone? The answer can reveal a lot about the user and his way of working; all crucial information.

By asking Joe a series of questions we can establish the background / context to his problem and document it; maybe something like this:

'Joe Bloggs is an unemployed civil engineer who lost his mobile phone while on a rock climbing expedition with his son. The phone fell from his pocket and shattered on a rock below – he was unable to retrieve any part of it. The phone is important to Joe as he uses it to communicate verbally with friends, send text messages and play a game called 'Kill the zombies'. He does not use the phone for business purposes. The phone he lost was an expensive 'smart' phone measuring 12cm by 7cm. The phone was not insured so Joe cannot claim a new phone on insurance. It was a 'pay as you go' phone, meaning Joe was not tied into a contract with a phone supplier. His wife sometimes used the phone to make private phone calls to her friends, but generally this was Joe's phone, which he used on a daily basis.

Joe needs to carry a mobile phone around with him at all times so that he can make a phone call if an emergency occurs, for example if he or his son fell during one of his rock climbing **expeditions**. *He also needs to log into the* *'kill the zombies' game on a daily basis to maintain his game point average in the game rankings. Sometimes he takes photographs with his phone of particularly beautiful scenery or rock formations.*

Joe now needs to replace the lost phone, but he only has limited funds. Ideally he would like to remain on a 'pay as you go' contract to avoid being tied into paying monthly contract fees. He would like the new phone to have the same functionality as the old phone but preferably with a faster processor so that the 'kill the zombies' game can load faster. His wife may also use the new phone on occasions to make phone calls. He would use the new phone at least as much as he does now, possibly more if it has new functionality that he finds useful'.

Four paragraphs of information is usually enough to establish the background and context. A more complicated problem may require more text, but as a guideline, try to stick to around four paragraphs. You want to describe the background without going into too much detail. You don't want to include irrelevant information, but on the other hand you do not want to miss anything useful. You don't want to write a novel, so try to keep it short and to the point. Because this is an iterative approach, you can always go back and amend the background as more information comes to light, or you can remove irrelevant information. Keep it high level and don't go into any real detail describing the problem or requirements. If useful detailed information regarding the problem and requirements comes out when talking to the users about the background and context, make sure you document it but keep it separate from the background text.

As a guideline, you are looking for a number of things to include in the background. These are the things you need to have documented:

- A general description of the problem area - including what's currently happening, what tools are currently being used etc.
- High level problem description - a very brief and high level description of the problem(s) that need to be addressed
- The objectives – high level overview of what needs to be achieved, and why. Make sure that you understand the objectives early on - you may need to revisit and expand on these later on.

You also need a list of stakeholders that you can work with during the analysis. We will come on to this in a minute.

Tool number one- Requirements Specification Template

Now, as an analyst you are likely to come across far more complicated problems than the one described here. In fact, throughout this book we are going to be looking at more complicated scenarios in order to illustrate how the approach can be used to simply and effectively deal with situations at any complexity level. Before we look at the background to a more complicated problem though, there is one more thing we need – some tools.

Every skilled practitioner needs a set of tools. A photographer uses a camera and lenses; an artist uses paints and easel. A business analyst uses numerous tools to get the job done, but there are three tools in particular that will be absolutely crucial when using this approach: templates, patterns and a good drawing or UML (unified modeling language) tool. To document the background (and subsequent information as we work through the approach) we are going to use a template – a requirements specification template. We will come on to the other two tools in later chapters.

One of the questions I am often asked is: why am I using a requirements specification template when there are numerous software tools available that will help manage requirements? The answer is simple... I am not trying to 'manage requirements' at this stage; I am conducting business analysis. The requirement management tools that are available commercially are generally designed to help an analyst document and manage their requirements i.e. allow them to view a set of requirements, track changes to those requirements, show relevant associations between requirements etc. We will come on to requirements management in a later chapter.

Using this approach you need to conduct analysis to build a good knowledge base first, before you begin documenting and managing requirements. The requirements specification template is a practical and easy way to record information about the knowledge base. You don't need any special tools, just a word processor that is capable of creating a template. All of the information about the knowledge base will be located in one place. It can be referenced and distributed to stakeholders easily for review. It can be easily updated and maintained. You can still manage a set of requirements in a separate requirement management tool, but you also need a document that can serve as a 'single point of truth' for the knowledge base that describes both the problem area and the needs for the solution.

The following is a good requirements specification template that we can use as a starting point:

Title:

Author:

Reviewer(s)

Change Log

Version	Date [DD-MMM-YYYY]	Description of changes
0.1		

Stakeholders

Name	Job Title	Role

Table of Contents:

Background:

Problem Statements:

Scope:
   In Scope:
   Out of scope:

Concept Diagram(s):

Business Use Case Diagram(s):

As Is Process Diagram(s):

To Be Process Diagram(s):

Activity Diagrams:

Change Requirements:

   Business Requirements:

ID	Requirements Description & Constraints	Priority	Status

   Functional Requirements:

Feature	ID	Requirements Description & Constraints	Priority	Status

   Non-Functional Requirements:

Feature	ID	Requirements Description & Constraints	Priority	Status

Business Rules:

Links to other documents:

Glossary:

Appendices:

The template is meant to be flexible i.e. if you need to record more information you can add additional headings. Likewise if you need less information you just remove what is not required. When using this approach it is important to only do what is necessary, no more and definitely no less, otherwise you will end up wasting valuable time.

If we were to continue with the Joe Bloggs phone replacement project, then we would need to complete the relevant sections of the requirements specification template as follows:

Title: Joe Bloggs Phone Replacement Project

Author: The author

Reviewer(s)

Change Log

Version	Date [DD-MMM-YYYY]	Description of changes
0.1	13-Oct-2015	Documented background

Stakeholders

Name	Job Title	Role
Joe Bloggs	Civil Engineer (unemployed)	Phone user

Table of Contents:

Background:

Joe Bloggs is an unemployed civil engineer who lost his mobile phone while on a rock climbing expedition with his son. The phone fell from his pocket and shattered on a rock below – he was unable to retrieve any part of it. The phone is important to Joe as he uses it to communicate verbally with friends, send text messages and play a game called 'Kill the zombies'. He does not use the phone for business purposes. The phone he lost was an expensive 'smart' phone measuring 12cm by 7cm. The phone was not insured so Joe cannot claim a new phone on insurance. It was a 'pay as you go' phone, meaning Joe was not tied into a contract with a phone supplier. His wife sometimes used the phone to make private phone calls to her friends, but generally this was Joe's phone, which he used on a daily basis.

Joe needs to carry a mobile phone around with him at all times so that he can make a phone call if an emergency occurs, for example if he or his son fell during one of his rock climbing expeditions. He also needs to log into the 'kill the zombies' game on a daily basis to maintain his game point average in the game rankings. Sometimes he takes photographs with his phone of particularly beautiful scenery or rock formations.

Joe now needs to replace the lost phone, but he only has limited funds to do so. Ideally he would like to remain on 'pay as you go' to avoid being tied into paying monthly contract fees. He would like the new phone to have the same functionality as the old phone but preferably with a faster processor so that the 'kill the zombies' game can load faster. His wife may also use the new phone on occasions to make phone calls. He would use the new phone at least as much as he does now, possibly more if it has new functionality that he finds useful'.

Stakeholders

I have mentioned the term 'stakeholder' a few times already but haven't actually said what a stakeholder is. A 'Stakeholder' is a person, group or organization who has an interest in the problem / work area. A stakeholder can be someone who provides the analyst with requirements but it can also be a project manager, a business sponsor, maybe even someone outside the organization. In referring to stakeholders, as an analyst you need to be primarily concerned with those stakeholders that can provide you with requirements. There are two main types of stakeholder who can do this:

- A 'user' i.e. someone who is actually going to use the solution. This type of stakeholder may use the solution directly, for example by inputting or extracting data from a system. Or the user might access the solution indirectly, for example by referring to information within the solution from another system.
- A subject matter expert (SME) i.e. someone who has expert knowledge of the domain area. This type of stakeholder may or may not actually be a user of the solution, but the knowledge that this person has is often invaluable to the business analyst.

If you are lucky, you will be provided with a list of the key stakeholders you will need to talk to when you begin work to establish the background to the issue. If you are not so lucky, this is the first thing you need to do as soon as you have a rough idea of the background. Identifying which stakeholders are able and willing to help you can be a challenge and may involve communicating with the business sponsor or manager, who would hopefully be able to recommend some people that you can talk to.

You need a representative set of business stakeholders (users and subject matter experts); ones who between them can cover the entire range of the work being discussed. Ideally, you want to keep your group of business stakeholders small. It is difficult to manage a large number of stakeholders in meetings, especially if they have diverging opinions. On the other hand, too few will not give a good representation. I have found the optimum number of business stakeholders to have in a meeting to be five… this number provides a good representation and will allow for some lively discussion!

Of course, if you are working on a large project then the number of interested stakeholders may well number in the hundreds or even thousands. You cannot talk to all of these stakeholders – you have to have a strategy in place to manage communication. You may want to set up a core group of stakeholders and make it the responsibility of this core group to communicate out to a wider audience. You may want to have several core groups of stakeholders e.g. one for each region if working on a global project. If you have a large number of stakeholders, employing a good communications manager (or communications team) becomes essential. Because communication is such a significant part of your job as a business analyst, it is absolutely crucial that you are directly involved with the communications manager / team (if there is one). Poor communication can kill a project, so make sure that the communication is handled correctly or at the very least, there are good communications channels open to the stakeholders.

Stakeholder Maps

Some analysts create stakeholder maps to identify characteristics or interest levels of the stakeholders. If you want to do this, go ahead; but I personally do not feel it is necessary, at least not for the analyst. Who is the stakeholder map for? Certainly not for the stakeholders! Show a stakeholder a map where that stakeholder is classified as having lots of influence but a low interest level and see how much co-operation you get from the stakeholder after that. The map is more likely to be a tool to help the project manager, so leave the stakeholder mapping to the project manager if he/she wants one. If you have a small group of stakeholders you will soon get to know their traits and interest levels in the project, you don't need a map to tell you this.

If you have a large group of stakeholders, as already stated, you will need to have a communication plan in place. You may or may not be involved in drawing up a stakeholder communication plan... this is often handled by one or more people on the project who have a specific role in handling stakeholder communication. For a large project, it is crucial that good communication with all stakeholders is put in place and handled properly i.e. the communication plan should be shared with all stakeholders. This will help set expectations and establish team trust. The project manager will most likely be involved in this task.

A stakeholder map is a political tool, relevant to the project manager who is in charge of a project and needs to know which stakeholders have the most influence; which ones will support the project and which ones will block it. As an analyst your relationship with the stakeholders (especially the users and SME's) should be to set up a good rapport with them; you need to work very closely with them, extract information from them and take them on the journey from where they are now to where they want to be in the future. The users are the ones with the problem and it is your job to work alongside and help them. You don't need a stakeholder map to do this.

One more thing about stakeholders – they usually have both a job title and a role and these are two completely different things. In our simple example regarding the lost phone, Joe Bloggs is an unemployed civil engineer. That's his job title. His job has absolutely nothing whatsoever to do with his phone... his phone is just a tool he uses on a day to day basis. As an analyst you don't need to be concerned with the job title, at least not with regards to the problem. You do however need to be concerned with the role that Joe is performing, because that role is directly related to the problem. Joe Bloggs role in this problem is as a 'phone user' – he uses a phone. This is a nice generic role and we can apply this role if need be to other problems where someone uses a phone, or other stakeholders who use this particular phone. We will be covering this in more detail later on, but for now just be aware that each stakeholder / user you deal with has both a job title and a role – these are two very different things and whatever you do don't get them mixed up - it's likely to cause some confusion!

The mathematical model problem

As a simplistic example, Joe Bloggs' lost phone is fine. In terms of a more realistic example, you are probably going to be dealing with multiple users. The users may be scattered all over the world. There may be multiple roles involved, there may even be multiple companies or organizations involved. Your problem may involve an existing system, a new system or even a number of new systems. It may involve process change or improvement, data migration, report generation, document management, organizational restructuring, storage and archiving, one project or multiple projects or even a huge program of work. Your problem might take a couple of weeks to deliver a solution, or it could take several years! It doesn't matter. Stick to the approach and you can deal with any of these situations.

Let's imagine then, that you have been called in to deal with a problem for Company X, a scientific company based in the United States. Company X is working with another organization – a University in Holland. They are working together to develop a mathematical model that measures certain properties of plants - a nice complicated system. Inputting data into this system is a laborious and manual process prone to user error – they want some improvements made to their existing system. The process they use to share data between the two organizations is unwieldy – looks like we might need to do some process improvement work here as well! Just to complicate things a little further, there are potential users in different countries and in different time zones, and the users probably have multiple roles.

Okay, so this is definitely more complicated than Joe's lost phone. The good news though, is that you have managed to secure a one hour interview with the sponsor. Now, how do you get the information you need to define the background out of the sponsor? What questions should you ask?

This first meeting is very important. You will obviously need to introduce yourself i.e. establish who you are and what your role is, maybe a brief introduction on what a business analyst does. You need to create a rapport with the users, so you need to show interest in the work. It always helps if you have some background knowledge of the domain area; it looks good if you've done some pre-reading about the issue. It also helps if you're someone who can type of write quickly... you will probably be bombarded with information and you need to capture as much of it as possible. Start off with something general like 'tell me about what you currently do and what issues you face..." This should (hopefully) trigger a tsunami of information.

I would heavily recommend that you make sure your users can see what you are writing. If you do this, the users can see the speed at which you are writing and will slow the flow of information to accommodate. The users can also easily correct you if you've captured something that is incorrect. I would also recommend you capture the information electronically and use a projector rather than use physical paper or whiteboards. This will save you having to retype everything electronically afterwards and avoid the need to translate handwriting that might need some interpretation...

Some of this information will need clarification, especially when it comes to acronyms or information that just doesn't make any sense because you are not familiar with the domain area. Try to slow things down, ask for clarification, ask for definition of acronyms, but just let them talk. Try to keep things focused on the main problem and try to steer the conversation so that you gain a good insight into the following key points:

1. What the current situation looks like
2. What the main problems are
3. What the objectives are

Let's imagine that you have now met with the sponsor in company X and he (or she) has given you lots of valuable information about the problem area. In fact, the sponsor hasn't just told you about the problem area, he (or she) has gone off on a complete tangent and told you lots of detailed information about the scientific studies being carried out as a result of the mathematical modeling, as well as some personal problems with managing the budget. However, you've done a good job of keeping the sponsor generally on track and you have enough information to come up with three or four paragraphs describing the background...

Background:

Company X is a global company based in the United States specializing in the evaluation of baculovirus pesticides that target one specific pest only. This type of pesticide is completely harmless to both other organisms and the Environment. Company X is working in collaboration with a Dutch University to develop a mathematical model which can simulate a spray of baculovirus onto a single cotton plant with the aim of examining the different factors affecting the efficacy of the spray. The model consists of three subsystems:

- *plant growth and architecture*
- *virus deposits and subsequent decay*
- *pest behavior*

A number of different parameters are currently being evaluated under both controlled glasshouse and field conditions in France and the results of the evaluations recorded and sent back to company X to feed into the mathematical model. In addition, the persistence of the baculovirus on the leaf surface will be evaluated, including the factors contributing to virus degradation i.e. intensity of UVB, effect of dew on leaf exudates and the effect of a protectant added to the PIB (polyhedral inclusion body containing virions).

Results from these evaluations are being sent back to the modelers on an ad hoc basis as the evaluations themselves can only be conducted if resource is available. Because the model is at an early stage of development, all results obtained from the evaluations are currently added manually into the model. The process for doing this is time consuming and prone to user error, even more so as some of the attributes necessary for data input do not yet exist, so these are being stored in spreadsheets outside the model.

Several outputs are required from the model, including the following:

- *a comparison of growth measurements of plants taken in France with those predicted by the model, over specific time intervals*
- *Measurement of number of PIBs remaining on leaf surface under field conditions compared to that predicted by the model*
- *A comparison of pest behavior under field conditions with that predicted by the model.*

These outputs are not currently generated from the model so the functionality to generate these outputs needs to be developed. The outputs also need to be shared with other interested parties in a format such that they can be re-used in evaluation reports and compared with other existing mathematical models.

Let's stop a minute and analyze exactly what we've written here. The first paragraph is describing Company X, what it does and its relationship with a Dutch University. The second paragraph is describing information that will feed into the tool (the model). Because the sponsor spoke at length about the science, we have included some references to this (but in a much condensed form!). The third paragraph describes some issues relating to process. Finally, the fourth paragraph is describing some objectives including new functionality that is required in the system and the ability to share data. We haven't included anything about the sponsor's budget management problems because, according to the sponsor when asked, it's not directly relevant to the mathematical modelling system. Our paragraphs are short and sparse on detail. Is this enough information? Does it give us a clear idea of exactly what's going on and what needs to be done? No, it doesn't, nor is it meant to. We can always go back and refine, add more detail, break it into sub-sections if need be. We may also need to describe all the strange and wonderful scientific terminology in a separate glossary – we'll come on to that in another chapter. What this does do though, is give us a good starting point.

The big picture

A very useful technique to use as part of your analysis early on is to obtain an overall view of where your particular piece of work fits in the overall landscape. Or in other words, where does your particular project fit in the 'big picture'? Is the piece of work you have been assigned part of something much larger? Where does the work you are involved with interact with other work that is being carried out? If you have been tasked to work on a project involving improvements to an existing system for company X, what other related work is company X doing that might have an impact on your project? What else is out there that your project will have an impact on?

You will find that very few projects are carried out completely in isolation. There is always a 'bigger picture'. The mathematical model example is probably only one element of an evaluation into the use of a baculovirus... there may well be more work going on that you are initially unaware of but that might prove very useful when helping to develop a solution.

Throughout your project you will need to make sure that you remain aware of the 'big picture'... all the other pieces of work, systems, stakeholders and potential sources of data that might impact on your own project. Sometimes you can gain some understanding of the big picture from talking to the users about their 'vision' - how do they see this piece of work operating in the future? Where will it fit in relation to other work, other systems? If you are working on a large program of work that may consist of multiple projects, you will need to dedicate some time up front to gaining a good understanding of this 'big picture'. You may want to create some simple context diagrams early on that describe the very high level processes that are carried out and the systems that are currently in use. One way of doing this is to use simple blocks in a diagram e.g.:

Processes & Systems:

Planning (planning tool)	Field Evaluations (Data Capture)	Modeling (modeling tool)	Analysis (statistics)	Recommendations (document management tool)

Often, your understanding of the big picture will become more developed as you gain knowledge of the current processes and issues that are relevant to your project. Always keep in mind the 'big picture' when working towards a solution...

Chapter 4 – Define the 'As Is' Process

You are still at the beginning of the approach. You have spent a little time talking to the sponsor or the initiator of the problem and you have a very rough idea regarding the background and context. You might have a rough idea about the problem(s) as well, but you certainly won't know if a) you have identified the real problem and b) if there are more problems lurking in the background that you are currently unaware of. Defining the 'As Is' process will help flush this out, as well as give you a much better understanding about what's currently going on, who's involved and what tools are currently being used. However, to get all the information you require from the 'As Is' process (which is basically a diagram describing the current way of working), you will need to map out the process steps in a very particular way. First though, you will need some sort of a drawing tool...

Tool number two – UML diagramming tool

I am going to suggest that you use a proper UML (unified modeling language) drawing tool for this, and there are a number of good reasons to do so. Yes, you can use something like Microsoft Visio, PowerPoint or even a piece of paper, but each of these tools has certain limitations that will make your job harder as we get into the detail. I would suggest you use a tool that can meet the following criteria:

- Simple and easy to use i.e. no steep learning curve
- Ability to create diagrams that are visually pleasing, easily understandable and extendable (across multiple pages if necessary – some diagrams can get very large)
- Ability to use unified modeling language objects in the diagrams so that the diagrams are standardized and acceptable to both users and developers
- Ability to re-use objects from a diagram without having to waste time recreating the same objects for use in another diagram
- Ability to share the diagrams with the users, but retain them as read only so that your users don't inadvertently (or deliberately) change them
- Ability to search for and access the diagrams quickly and efficiently
- Ability to add notations to the diagrams. This is extremely important and you'll see why as we describe the creation of the 'As Is' process diagram
- Ability to create process diagrams, use case diagrams and data diagrams from within the tool

There are a number of UML tools available, but for this approach you only need to create three types of diagram, so I would suggest you don't waste time and money purchasing an expensive UML tool. There are some extremely powerful and useful open source UML tools available that can meet all of the criteria above and more, but the one I would recommend personally (and will be using in the examples throughout this book) is a tool called 'StarUML'. It is available for download here:

http://staruml.io/download

The latest version of StarUML is a very good tool with an attractive modern interface, but it is not freeware. If you want to use it for commercial purposes you will need to purchase a license. The license is not expensive and the software is well supported and updated on a regular basis. However, if you don't mind the retro look and feel of an older interface and you want to save some money on license costs, it may still be possible to download version 1 (although it has been out of support since 2008). Version 1 is completely free and works fine (currently) on computers running the latest version of Microsoft Windows which at time of writing is Windows 10. It is not as elegant as the later version, but it does the job.

If you need more information about UML I would also recommend Scott Kendall's book 'UML Explained'. There are many books describing what UML is and how to use it, so I will not repeat that information here... we are going to concentrate solely on the approach.

Creating the As Is Process diagram

Now that we have a tool, let's open it up and start drawing! Now, I'm not going to explain how to use the tool... I'm going to leave this up to you to figure out, especially as the tool you are using may not be the UML tool I am recommending. Suffice to say, if you are using a UML tool then you will need to create a new 'Activity' diagram to draw the process. In UML, an activity diagram is used to describe workflows. You should see an activity represented by a round edged rectangle e.g.

We will be using this icon to represent the process steps in the 'As Is' process.

There are a few more icons that you need to be aware of, that we will be using for this diagram:

This little filled circle represents the start of the process. Generally, there should only be one of these on your diagram, unless your process is triggered by multiple diverse inputs.

This filled circle with another circle drawn around it represents an end point in your process. Again, you should only have one end point on your diagram unless the process involves multiple diverse outputs.

This triangle represents a decision point. You may have multiple decision points in your diagram.

You will be using arrows to join one icon to another icon to represent the direction of process flow (as above)

This is a 'swim lane.' The swim lane represents a 'role' e.g. 'phone user'. All of the activities and decision points need to be drawn within a swim lane. The arrows can cross swim lanes. The start and the end points need to be outside the swim lanes. The swim lane can be drawn vertically or horizontally – I tend to use horizontal swim lanes but this is more or less personal preference.

Finally, the only other icon you will need in your drawing is this one… the notation or 'note'. Notes should be attached to activities via a dotted line e.g.

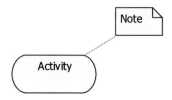

One activity can have multiple notes associated with it.

This is really all you need for a process diagram… you can safely ignore all the other UML artifacts for the moment.

The phone problem revisited

Ok, let's begin with Joe Bloggs and his phone problem. For each aspect of the approach we will generally start with the simple problem, show the theory behind what we're trying to do, and then apply it to the more complicated problem. Joe Bloggs currently has no phone, so if he wants to make a phone call he needs to either borrow someone else's phone or find a telephone box. He can't play his favorite game and he can't send text messages without a phone, so his current ('As Is') process is going to start off looking something like this:

Fig. 4 – 'As Is' process for using a phone

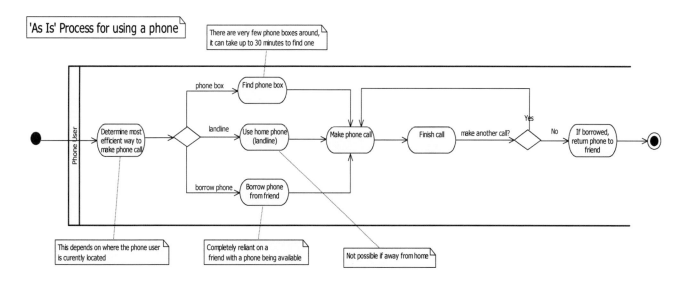

Now, even though this is a small diagram, it's virtually unreadable on the page due to its size. Normally, you would share this diagram electronically with instructions to view it at between 200% to 400% zoom, so that the text is fully readable. For now though, I'm going to show the diagram in two parts to make it readable and comment separately on each part:

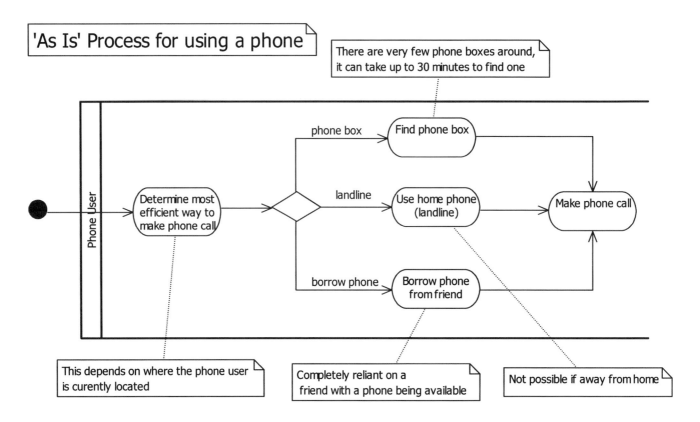

Fig. 5 - part 1 of the 'As Is' diagram for using a phone:

Ok, we have a start point, where the trigger (the initiating event) for the entire process occurs. It is often useful to define what this trigger is, especially if there are multiple triggers occurring in the process, but in this example we haven't defined what the trigger is. It's important to note that this process diagram is being created primarily for you, the business analyst, more than for the users. The users already know what they're doing (or at least you would hope they do!) whereas you are using this diagram to understand what it is they currently do. So if you find describing the trigger useful, put it in the diagram. In this case the trigger would be something like 'phone user wants to make a phone call' so on the line joining the start point with the first process you could write 'need to make phone call' or something similar.

The next point to make is that the text in the activity box is just describing 'what' is happening, not how. So the first activity – 'determine most efficient way to make phone call' – describes WHAT the phone user is doing. Don't mention anything to do with software tools in the activity; keep it short and sweet, make it very clear and understandable – use a verb e.g. 'determine', 'find', 'borrow', 'use' etc. Keep it fairly high level as well – don't go into the intricate details unless it's absolutely necessary. In this example we have an activity called 'make phone call' and that's sufficient; you don't need to describe activities such as 'pick up receiver', 'listen for dial tone', 'input telephone number' etc. Sure, these are all part of the process, but unless the stakeholder mentions one of these detailed sub-activities as being particularly important, leave it out. Otherwise your diagram will explode into something completely unmanageable.

On the other hand, make sure that you do include sufficient detail so that you have a clear idea about what's happening. You do not want a process diagram that is so high level it hides all of the issues. What do I mean by too high level? Here's the same example, at too high a level:

Fig. 6 - High level process diagram

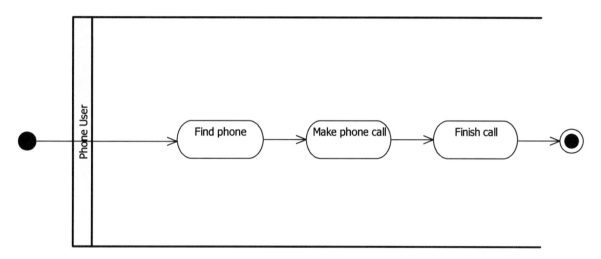

Looking at the above diagram, where are the issues? What is the problem? It all looks pretty straightforward and it tells you virtually nothing. Do not try to hide complexity for the sake of simplifying the diagram – this diagram is going to be absolutely key to your understanding. If there is complexity in the process, make sure that you show it. I'll say it again; the 'As Is' diagram is primarily for the business analyst. It is a tool for enabling the analyst to understand the current ways of working and it also serves as a means of communication with stakeholders. If the diagram shows lots of issues and complexity then that's fine because that is what is currently happening and you need to understand the current situation before you can move to a future state.

We've talked a lot about the 'what' here… we also need to know about the 'how'. 'Determine most efficient way to make phone call' - how is the phone user carrying out this process step? Maybe he does this by tossing a coin, maybe he spends 20 minutes in meditation before reaching a decision… you may or may not need to know this information but if you do, don't write it in the activity box! This is extremely important – make sure that all the activities describe only 'what' is happening and not how. These activities are directly related to the functionality that is required and it will be very easy later on to work out what the functionalities are if the processes all describe the 'what'.

You will generally find that many of the problems, including different ways of working, are usually based on 'how' things are done rather than on 'what' is done. Documenting the 'how' is crucial to understanding the problems, which we will come on to in the next chapter. Documenting the 'what' is crucial to understanding the functionality needed and the requirements. Mixing the 'what' and the 'how' can really complicate things and make the description of what is actually happening very unclear. I will emphasize this point again - you need to keep the 'what' and the 'how' separate.

How do you keep the 'what' and the 'how' separate but still show both on the same diagram? You use the notation – the notes. Try to write a note for each process step. Within the note, describe exactly what the user tells you about this process step – how the step is carried out, what tools are used, how long it takes, any interactions with other stakeholders, what the issues are… try to keep these notes short and concise (see fig. 5 for some examples). If there is a lot of information to be recorded for a particular process step, break it down… any identified problems and requirements can be documented in the requirements specification document so don't include these in the notes; put them straight into the document. You could if you like, write notes separate to the diagram e.g. you could create a process diagram describing 'what' is happening and a separate list or table of notes describing the 'how'. The 'how' would also include references to tools used and any identified issues for each process step. If you prefer to do it this way then that's absolutely fine; I personally find it a real pain to have to number each process and cross correlate notes with each process step – I find it much easier to view everything on one diagram.

We have a decision point in the diagram. You can use these to show different options as I've done in this example, or you can use them to show different paths taken dependent on a yes / no answer.

Here's the rest of the process diagram for completeness:

Fig. 7 - part 2 of the 'As Is' diagram for using a phone:

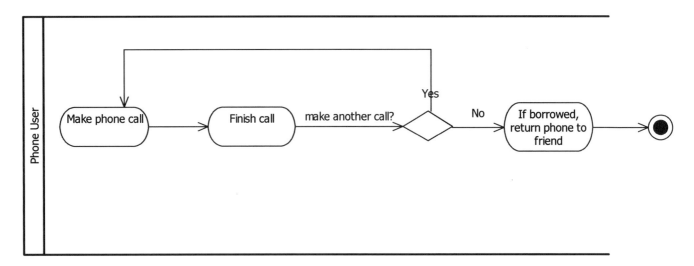

In this section of the diagram I have a decision point showing yes / no paths. I have described the question leading to the yes / no answer on the line leading to the decision point. If you are using a different tool you could write the question on or in the decision point itself. The process has a clear end point. If you like, you could add text to the line leading to the end point describing the output or state at which the process finishes e.g. 'phone call completed'. The advantage of doing this is that it could become the trigger for another process… if you have a very complicated scenario with multiple process diagrams they may be linked by an output from one process becoming the trigger for another.

The only other thing of note in this part of the process diagram is the final step – 'if borrowed, return phone to friend'. I have included an 'if' statement in this step rather than another decision point asking if the phone was borrowed or not. I did this for convenience, because I thought adding another decision point was unnecessary and because it's pretty clear. A real stickler for the rules of process mapping could probably find fault with the way some of this diagram is laid out or the use of the notes, but to be honest you really don't need to create the perfect diagram following all of the rules… you just need to create something that does the job. That job is to ensure you have a good understanding of the current way the users are working, the tools that they are using and the issues they currently have. If you can obtain this clear understanding by using a single diagram then you will have succeeded!

The mathematical problem revisited

The chances of having a single role with a nice process flow are slim, but it does happen. More likely though is that there are multiple roles with the process flow crossing back and forth across the roles. There may be circumstances where a single activity is carried out by multiple roles working together. You may receive a mass of information from the users regarding how they carry out one particular activity and virtually nothing about another activity. The users may go into too much detail when describing the process, or too little detail. All of these things (and more) can happen, so let's take a quick look at how we can deal with some of this using a more complicated example.

Let's revisit the background describing the mathematical model problem from chapter 3:

Background:

Company X is a global company based in the United States specializing in the evaluation of baculovirus pesticides that target one specific pest only. This type of pesticide is completely harmless to both other organisms and the Environment. Company X is working in collaboration with a Dutch University to develop a mathematical model which can simulate a spray of baculovirus onto a single cotton plant with the aim of examining the different factors affecting the efficacy of the spray. The model consists of three subsystems:

- *plant growth and architecture*
- *virus deposits and subsequent decay*
- *pest behavior*

A number of different parameters are currently being evaluated under both controlled glasshouse and field conditions in France and the results of the evaluations recorded and sent back to company X to feed into the mathematical model. In addition, the persistence of the baculovirus on the leaf surface will be evaluated, including the factors contributing to virus degradation i.e. intensity of UVB, effect of dew on leaf exudates and the effect of a protectant added to the PIB (polyhedral inclusion body containing virions).

Results from these evaluations are being sent back to the modelers on an ad hoc basis as the evaluations themselves can only be conducted if resource is available. Because the model is at an early stage of development, all results obtained from the evaluations are currently added manually into the model. The process for doing this is time consuming and prone to user error, even more so as some of the attributes necessary for data input do not yet exist, so these are being stored in spreadsheets outside the model.

Several outputs are required from the model, including the following:
- *a comparison of growth measurements of plants taken in France with those predicted by the model, over specific time intervals*
- *Measurement of number of PIBs remaining on leaf surface under field conditions compared to that predicted by the model*
- *A comparison of pest behavior under field conditions with that predicted by the model.*

These outputs are not currently generated from the model so the functionality to generate these outputs needs to be developed. The outputs also need to be shared with other interested parties in a format such that they can be re-used in evaluation reports and compared with other existing mathematical models.

Let's also imagine that we have now managed to identify who some of the key stakeholders are:

Stakeholders

Name	Job Title	Role
Martin White	Mathematical Modeler (UK)	Modeler
Jan Von deGroot	Mathematical Modeler (NL)	Modeler
Pierre LeBlanc	Field Trial Coordinator (FR)	
Jean Vert	Field trial assistant (FR)	
Gerald Black	Senior Scientist (USA)	
Patricia Brun	Data analyst (USA)	

Talking to the stakeholders

So, we have users from several European countries and two based in the USA. We know their job titles but we are unclear on their exact roles. By talking to these individuals about what they currently do, either in a single meeting with all of them present (preferred) or in individual meetings, we should be able to determine what the rest of the roles are.

The advantage of having multiple stakeholders in a single meeting is that you will receive input that could trigger discussion. For example if individuals do not agree on what their process is, the group can share and come to a common understanding. If multiple people in the same role do the same thing using different tools or in different ways, good discussion will ensue. This sort of information sharing can be crucial in identifying potential issues. Be aware though, that managing a meeting with six people talking about what they currently do can easily get out of hand, especially if you have some strong personalities in the meeting. This is where all your skills at asking the right questions, stopping the discussion going off on tangents and summarizing what you've just heard to clarify your own understanding, come to the fore.

Again, try to draw the diagram electronically in the meeting with the stakeholders so that they can see it taking shape as they talk. This also serves as a check to make sure that you have understood what they have told you and that you have documented it correctly. If your users / subject matter experts are in remote locations, use teleconferencing and share your screen via one of the video conferencing tools such as Skype. Don't try to draw everything out perfectly. It doesn't matter if your diagram looks messy; you can always clean it up later. One other thing – always draw your diagrams from left to right or from top to bottom and try to avoid crossing lines - it makes things much easier to read.

The first questions you need to ask are:

- What is the first thing that happens?
- What is triggering this activity?
- Which role is responsible for carrying out this initial activity?

One of the most common things that happen at the beginning of a process is that someone, possibly external, is initiating the whole thing by a request for something or a request to do something. This could be described on the diagram as a trigger (i.e. an initiating event) or to get things started you could draw it on the diagram as the first activity. Once you have a starting point and your first activity is drawn on the diagram, you need to talk a little about that activity.

- How is this activity currently carried out?
- What tools (if any) are used?
- Are there any problems with carrying out this particular activity?
- What happens next?

And you keep repeating this line of questioning for every activity that follows. Often, you will need to ask for more information or clarification about a particular activity. Be particularly careful when the process flow crosses to a new role - you will need to ask about how communication happens between the two roles as communication between roles is often a common pain point.

Depending on the answers, you may get something that looks like this:

Fig. 8 – describing the first part of the process:

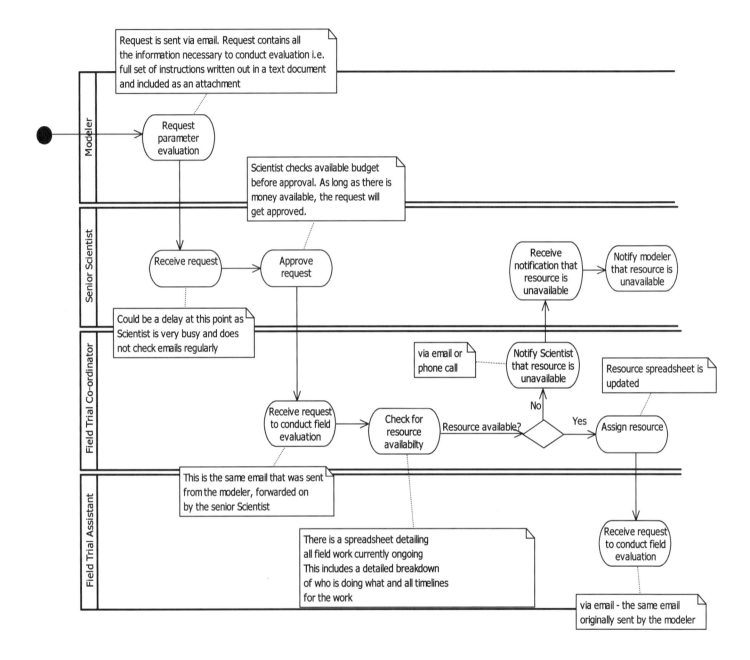

Now, there are a number of important points of note here.

1. We are using exactly the same technique that we used for the lost phone problem in that we have processes describing the 'what', notes describing the 'how', decision points and roles. The difference here is that we have more roles…

2. We have used job titles for some of the roles. At the moment this doesn't really matter… we can change this once we have a clearer idea of what is happening in the process. For example the Senior Scientist might become an 'Approver', the field trial co-ordinator might become a 'resource manager' etc.

3. Because we included the field trials role in the meeting as well as the modelers, we are obtaining information that may not actually be in scope of the work that was originally requested. If the focus of the work (in this example) needs to be on the input of results into the model and the generation of output from the model, maybe the inclusion of the parameter evaluation part of the process (where the issue of resource occurs) is irrelevant? However, by excluding these stakeholders we would be making an assumption – that the conducting of the parameter evaluations is outside the scope of the work. This may well be true, but it's an assumption and rule number 2 says 'beware of assumptions'! So we include these stakeholders for three reasons: a) to obtain the 'big picture', b) because an issue with resource was mentioned in the background and c) to ensure we are not making an incorrect assumption. It is often worth stepping back a little and obtaining a wider overview, looking at the 'big picture'; in order to have a clearer understanding of where the issues occur and putting them into context.

4. The level of detail we are working at here is potentially revealing other issues that are alluded to but not specifically described in the background. For example, a delay in approving the request might mean that resource is already allocated before the trials co-ordinator receives the request. Is using a spreadsheet the best way to manage resource? We could dig a little deeper here if need be… where is this spreadsheet stored? Who has access to it? Who needs to have access to it? This spreadsheet wasn't mentioned during the session with the project sponsor so it may be completely out of scope. However, we may have identified a potential pain point in the process that might be related to the resourcing issue and may need further investigation.

5. Again, because we have included the parameter evaluation in the process, we may end up with a very large diagram that actually deals with two separate processes: 'Evaluate model parameters' and 'Conduct modeling work'. It may well be better to split this into two diagrams – one dealing with the conducting of the field work to obtain parameter data and the other dealing with the process for using that data in the model and generating output.

Let's take a quick look at what the end section of the process might potentially look like:

Fig. 9 – the end section of the process

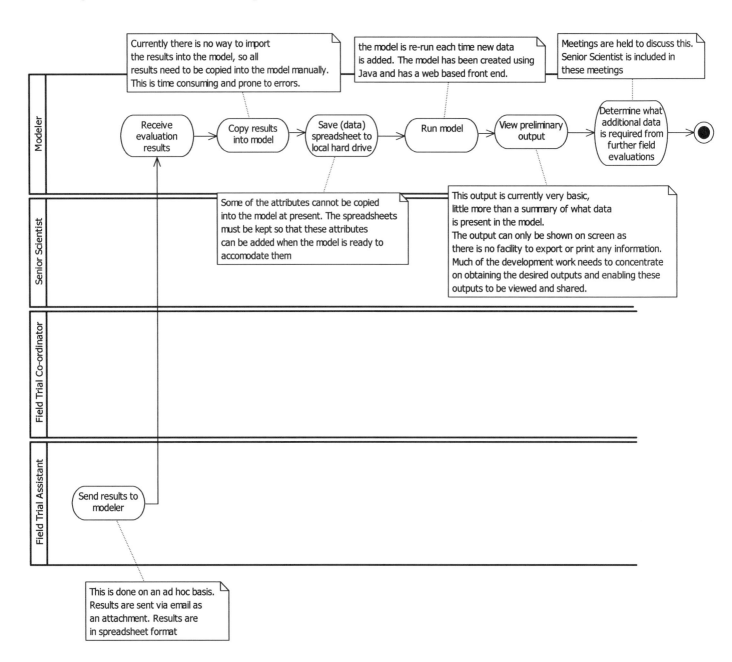

There are a couple of additional points to note here:

1. We have actually kept this latter part of the diagram very high level. We have not gone into much technical detail regarding how the model is run, although we have included a note stating which software was used to build it. This is deliberate... the technical details for such a model may be very complicated and we are still at an early stage in our understanding. The question you need to ask yourself is... will knowing the intricate details of how the software

currently operates help with defining the process? The answer is... it depends. Anything that might put constraints on the solution is useful information; hence the note about what software was used to build the model. If there is an elaborate process involved in running the software then that might also be worth recording, especially if that process highlights a problem. You might even need a detailed activity diagram describing the operation of the software if this is where the core of the problem lies! However, it is very easy to become bogged down with technical details when defining the 'As Is' process. Your users may be enthusiastic about the product they are using and want to explain how it works; they may want to give you a demonstration of it as well. You can always revisit the detail if required – just make sure you describe the As Is process sufficiently to gain a good understanding of what is happening and try to avoid getting bogged down in the detail!

2. The second point to note is that there is an activity right at the end of the process where multiple users are involved (Determine what additional data is required from further field evaluations). The temptation might be to try to expand the activity box so that it crosses multiple swim lanes, but I would recommend you avoid doing this. The reason why is because this will only work if the activity is carried out by roles that are in adjacent swim lanes. If you have another role in between the two roles that are carrying out the activity, the activity will appear to be carried out by all three roles and this would be incorrect. It is also possible that an activity may involve several different roles, some of which may not even be on the diagram. Rather than add these roles to the diagram (there could be a lot of roles and only one relevant activity) it is far better just to record in a note that the activity is being carried out by multiple roles and list the roles involved. A typical example of this situation is when a meeting is held that involves multiple roles.

Scenarios where people are using different processes to achieve the same goal

There are going to be times when you will be working with multiple groups of stakeholders, all of whom are trying to achieve the same goal or objective, but in different ways. This might occur for example when you are dealing with users based in different countries or in different organizational groups. The key goal or objective for what they are doing may be the same but the operational process for getting there may well be different. In situations like this you may need to meet separately with each group of users and document each of their 'As Is' processes in multiple diagrams. You will end up with several 'As Is' process diagrams, one for each group of users. You then have a choice; you could try to combine the process diagrams into one higher level generic process diagram highlighting the differences between the user groups, or you could just include all the multiple diagrams in your requirements specification document as they are. The benefit of creating a generic diagram (if you can) and highlighting where the differences occur in notes is that everything is visible from the one diagram. The downside is that the notes can make the diagram very confusing and possibly inaccurate. If the processes are very different, it may not be possible to create a generic diagram.

Here is a very simple example showing two separate processes for making a cup of tea, along with a generic high level process diagram showing both processes with the differences highlighted on the diagram:

Fig. 10 – 'As Is' process for making a cup of tea using a teapot:

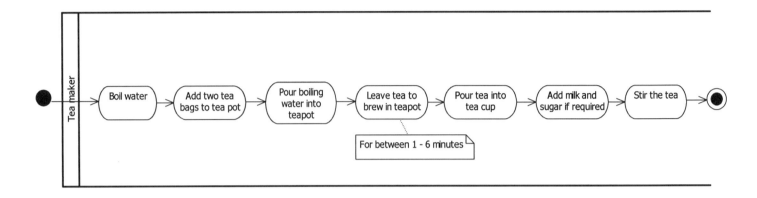

Fig. 11 – 'As Is' process for making a cup of tea with a teabag:

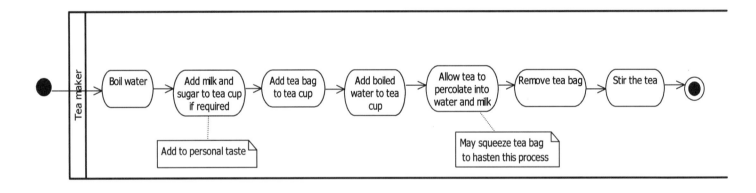

Fig. 12 – Generic 'As Is' process for making a cup of tea:

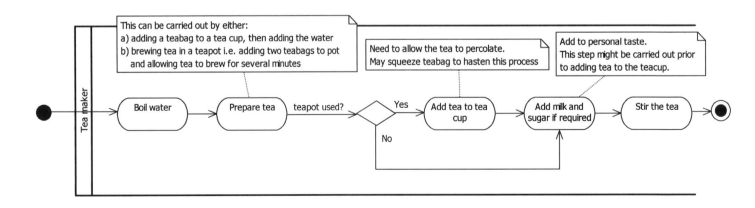

Of course there are lots of different variations for the process of making a cup of tea, including the very intricate Japanese tea ceremony process. If you tried to draw a diagram for every variation you would end up with an awful lot of diagrams! There may be times when you really need the different diagrams to show the process variations and there may be times when you can get away with a generic diagram. Generally speaking, if you have processes with fairly minor differences you can probably get away with creating a generic 'As Is' diagram. Often you will have to use your judgment and decide if multiple diagrams are really necessary.

Finally, apart from gaining a good understanding of what your users are currently doing, the 'As Is' process is also an excellent means of identifying and discussing issues that will end up in your requirements specification document as problem statements. It will enable you to identify many of the key concepts (terminology) that are being used by the stakeholders. It will also serve as the starting point for defining the key functionalities that will later be used to help define the 'To Be' process. Which brings us nicely to the end of this chapter and leads us on to the next step in the approach…

Chapter 5 – Create Initial Problem Statements

Now that you have an 'As Is' process diagram describing what the users are currently doing, you should be in a good position to work on some initial problem statements. It is highly likely that during the time you spent with the users / subject matter experts discussing both the background and the 'as Is' process, some of the problems experienced would have also been discussed. In this chapter we will concentrate on how we go about analyzing and documenting the problem statements. Firstly though, what exactly is a 'problem statement'?

Wikipedia has a pretty good description of what a problem statement is:

'A brief description of the issues that need to be addressed by a problem solving team and should be presented to them (or created by them) before they try to solve the problem'.

Interestingly enough, there are not many books on business analysis out there that go into much (if any) detail about writing problem statements and why they are needed. So let's rectify that by saying straight off that problem statements are vitally important. **You should not be working on a solution to a problem if you do not know what the problem is that you are trying to address.** Amazingly enough, this is a very common error and must be one of the main reasons why many projects fail. You need to have a good understanding of what the problems are that you're trying to address, but actually defining what those problems are can sometimes be very difficult. This is why this chapter is called 'create *initial* problem statements' with the emphasis on 'initial'… more work will be needed as you progress through the approach to refine these problem statements and define the root cause of the problems.

Something else to quickly note here… Requirements and problems are two completely different things. You could in theory have a solution in place that meets all the requirements, but if the solution does not address the fundamental problems then it's not going to be a good solution and may not even be used. The requirements come later… much later. Do not try to document the requirements at this stage… you have an 'As Is' process and some background information about the piece of work you've been assigned to, but all that gives you is a clearer understanding of what your users currently do and some of the issues that they've highlighted. If they start giving you requirements, you need to ask them what the issue is behind that requirement - what problem is that requirement trying to address?

Defining problem statements up front gives you several important advantages:

1. Problem statements provide the justification for doing the work. Why would you be doing the work in the first place if not to address some fundamental problem? Defining the problems up front enables your sponsor or project manager to draw up a good business case for obtaining funding – they can use these problem statements as part of the business case.
2. Problem statements can help identify areas where improvements can be made. When the iPad was launched onto the market in 2010 it became an instant success because it addressed some

fundamental issues with existing tablet computers in terms of design and user experience (Apples' excellent marketing strategy didn't do it any harm either!).

3. Problem statements keep you focused on areas that are important. If for example you have a system that needs updating and a lot of requirements; knowing what the issues are with the system enables you to focus primarily on those issues and this focus helps with prioritizing the requirements.

4. Problem statements will help you define the objectives for the piece of work you are involved with. If you have a set of problems that need addressing, your objectives should correlate to the problems. As we will see later, problems can be linked to objectives which can be linked to business requirements, which can be linked to functional requirements… everything in this approach is actually linked to everything else…

When you speak to the users about the background and their current ways of working, you will at the same time be trying to make a note of any issues or problems that the users have. These notes are your initial source of information for documenting the problem statements. Your users are highly unlikely to give you nicely phrased, accurate and concise problem statements though. If you are very lucky they will tell you what the real problem is, but they are far more likely to tell you what they think they need, or they will tell you what they *think* the problem is. On the surface what they say might sound quite plausible, but on the other hand what they say might be obtuse or perhaps completely misleading. This is where rule number 2 really comes into its own. Beware of assumptions! When a user tells you what the problem is… take it with a pinch of salt. Yes, it probably is a problem, but what is causing that problem? Why is it a problem? Write it down, verbatim if you like, but make sure that you have captured what it is the user thinks is the problem. Be prepared to do some follow-up analysis afterwards!

Documenting the problems

There are quick and easy ways to document the problems as well as more convoluted methods. As this is an 'agile' (in terms of efficiency) as well as an iterative approach, we will stick to a quick and easy way of writing a problem statement and avoid the long drawn out ways that involves lots of descriptive text and analysis. A quick and easy way of writing a problem statement is to just write it down as one or two sentences of text. And that's it… keep it simple… for now. You do need to make sure that you write sufficient information to ensure that the problem statement is understandable to all the stakeholders, so avoid using acronyms, ambiguous terminology or anything that might lead to confusion. Make sure that what you have written is clear, unambiguous and precise. In fact this advice applies to everything that you document, including names of process steps, names of use cases and of course, requirements. We need to do some further analysis work with these sentences, but we'll come to that in a minute.

For now though, let's go back to our first simple example with the phone and Joe Bloggs. What has he told us about his problems? We do have some information we can use from documenting the background and the 'As Is' process:

1. He's unemployed.

2. He doesn't have much money.
3. He's lost his phone.
4. His phone wasn't insured.
5. He can't play his 'kill the zombies' game.
6. He can't send text messages.
7. He has trouble making phone calls - currently he has to use a phone box to make phone calls and it can take him up to half an hour to find a phone box or he has to borrow a phone from a friend.
8. He can't take photographs of beautiful scenery or rock formations.
9. Even when he had his phone, it was slow to load the 'kill the zombies' game.
10. If he had more useful functionality built into his phone then he might use the phone more.

Ok, Joe Bloggs has a lot of problems! Not all of these are relevant to his phone either. We've written all these 'problems' down… they could be deemed problem statements in themselves but how many of these are 'real' problems? What I mean by this is - what's actually causing these problems? If you identify the cause of a problem, you will have identified the 'real' problem, the actual issue that needs to be tackled. Some of these problems may be 'real' problems and some may just be the result of an effect caused by an underlying problem. The job now is to find out which is which.

One of the most effective ways to get to the 'real' underlying problem is to use a technique called 'root cause analysis', which basically means identifying the root cause of a problem. One of the most effective ways to perform root cause analysis is to keep asking the question 'why' until you get to a point where you're pretty certain you have the 'real' problem documented. Usually you should not need to ask the question 'why?' more than five times to get to the root cause of a problem. Why doesn't Joe Bloggs have much money? Because he doesn't have a job or in other words, because he is unemployed. We could ask the question 'why doesn't he have a job?" but that would only help if we were trying to address a problem regarding Joe's state of employment, so a single 'why' will suffice in this case.

So having documented some simple (but clear and unambiguous) problem statements, you can then review each statement with the users / subject matter experts and perform some basic root cause analysis for each statement. Or you might want to do this at a later point in time… after all we're still gathering information at this stage and more issues and problems might come to light as we talk to the users about concepts and functionalities.

For the purposes of this book however, we are going to do the analysis on these problems straight away. The first thing to do is to put these problem statements into a three column table:

Fig. 13 – a three column problem statement table:

ID	Problem	Root cause
1	Joe Bloggs doesn't have much money	Joe Bloggs is unemployed
2	Joe Bloggs phone wasn't insured	Joe Bloggs is unemployed
3	Joe Bloggs can't play his 'kill the zombies' game	Joe Bloggs has lost his phone
4	Joe Bloggs can't send text messages	Joe Bloggs has lost his phone
5	Joe Bloggs has trouble making phone calls - currently he has to use a phone box to make phone calls and it can take him up to half an hour to find a phone box or he has to borrow a phone from a friend.	Joe Bloggs has lost his phone
6	Joe Bloggs can't take photographs of beautiful scenery or rock formations	Joe Bloggs has no access to a camera
7	Even when Joe had his phone, it was slow to load the 'kill the zombies' game	Old phone used a slow processor
8	If he had more useful functionality built into his phone then he might use the phone more	Old phone didn't provide extra functionality that is available in a more modern phone

Giving each problem an identifier can be useful, especially if you want to map these problems to objectives and requirements later on. The second column describes the problem itself and the third column specifies the root cause of the problem. You can see instantly from the above that several problems may be due to a single root cause. The fact that Joes Bloggs doesn't have much money is down to him being unemployed. His phone wasn't insured because he doesn't have enough money to insure it, which is because he's unemployed. He can't play his game or send text messages because his phone is lost. He is forced to use alternative means to make phone calls because he's lost his phone. He can't take photographs because he doesn't have access to a camera. Losing the phone is not the root cause of this problem, because if he had access to a camera he would still be able to take photographs. His game was slow to load because of the speed of the processor in his old phone. Finally, number 8 is not really a problem, more an opportunity. We've turned this into a problem though so that it can be addressed…

If you have a lot of problems you might want to add a fourth column, between the ID and the problem. Call this column 'Process' or 'Process Step' and use it to break your problems down by process step. This is particularly useful for relating the problems back to the 'As Is' process from where they probably originated. We can use this format for the example describing the more complicated problem involving the mathematical model e.g.

Fig. 14 – a four column problem statement table:

ID	Process step	Problem	Root cause
1	Approve request	Approval of request can take several days to process	Checking for requests in email is low priority compared to other work conducted by Senior Scientist
2	Approve request	Request can get 'lost' in email system	Checking for requests in email is low priority compared to other work conducted by Senior Scientist
3	Approve request	It takes up to an hour to check the available budget	Available budget is not readily available to view
4	Check for resource availability	Resource is often already allocated elsewhere before the request is received	Delay in receiving request due to approval process

By adding this additional column to the table we have enabled categorization of problems by process step. This gives us a direct link between process and problem, which has several significant benefits:

- We can establish a direct series of links from the process, to the problems experienced within the process, and later to the requirements needed to address the problems. This will serve as a nice check (during the development phase) to make sure that all the problems that need to be addressed are actually being addressed.

- We can use this information to help define the scope (what is in scope and what is outside the scope) as it triggers the questions: is this process within scope? If so, which of the problems within this process need to be addressed? How important is it that these problems get addressed?

- Laying out the problems in this manner makes it easier to prioritize what needs to be done

- As we have the root cause documented alongside the problem we can ask the question: 'will addressing the root cause of the problem actually solve the problem?' You would like to think so, but there may be situations where this is not actually the case; either the root cause isn't absolutely correct or addressing the root cause leads to further (unforeseen?) problems…this can be another valuable check.

- We can use this information to help define the 'To Be' process (you'll see how later)

Note that I've added the information about the role in the column describing the process step – this gives the advantage of knowing which role has the problem. Alternatively you can create an additional column in the table to specifically record the role; this will allow you to pivot the table to view problems by role (if you export the table into a spreadsheet tool). Another useful additional column that you might consider adding is a 'priority' column – that way you can record a priority against each of the problems and view all the information in the table at a glance - what the problem is, who has the problem, where the problem occurs in the process, how important the problem is, what the root cause of the problem is… all very useful information!

Chapter 6 – Define the Business Concepts

Assuming you've got the background documented, a reasonable 'As Is' process and made a start on the problem statements, you should be well on the way to gaining a good understanding of what is currently happening with regards the particular piece of work that you have been tasked to analyze. This chapter is going to concentrate on building a business concept model, which is a very useful diagram that will help clarify your understanding of the work area and provide the foundation for understanding some of the data needs.

If you are already familiar with entity relationship diagrams, a business concept diagram is virtually the same thing. An entity–relationship diagram (model) describes inter-related things of interest for a specific domain of knowledge. A business concept model also describes inter-related things of interest within the knowledge domain. When you create a business concept model you are effectively creating an entity relationship model. The terms 'business concept' and 'entity' can be regarded as being synonymous. The only reason I am calling this diagram a 'business concept diagram' (or model) as opposed to an entity relationship diagram is because I want to emphasize the point that this diagram is only being used to describe business concepts and not data items. We cannot easily start describing data needs at such an early stage in the process, mainly because we are still trying to understand the current ways of working. However, we can begin identifying the business concepts that may later be used to define the data items needed in the future.

Now, what I mean by a business concept is an object or thing or piece of information, something tangible that is used within the business (knowledge) domain. A 'house' is a business concept. A 'wall' within the house is another business concept. In our simple example with Joe Bloggs, the 'phone' is a good example of a business concept. It's a thing, an object, used by Joe. 'Phone' is a business concept. A business concept can have 'attributes' or properties. An 'attribute' (or 'property') is a quality or feature belonging to a concept (or entity). If 'house' is a business concept, one of the attributes (properties) of a house might be shape, or colour.

What other business concepts are there in the Joe Bloggs example, and how do we identify them? Let's take another look at the background we've written for the Joe Bloggs example:

Joe Bloggs is an unemployed civil engineer who lost his **mobile phone** while on a rock climbing expedition with his son. The **phone** fell from his pocket and shattered on a rock below – he was unable to retrieve any part of it. The phone is important to Joe as he uses it to communicate verbally with friends, send **text messages** and play a **game** called '**Kill the zombies**'. He does not use the phone for business purposes. The phone he lost was an expensive **'smart' phone** measuring 12cm by 7cm. The phone was not insured so Joe cannot claim a new phone on insurance. It was a **'pay as you go' phone**, meaning Joe was not tied into a **contract** with a **phone supplier**. His wife sometimes used the phone to make private phone calls to her friends, but generally this was Joe's phone, which he used on a daily basis.

Joe needs to carry a mobile phone around with him at all times so that he can make a **phone call** if an emergency occurs, for example if he or his son fell during one of his rock climbing expeditions. He also needs to log into the 'kill the zombies' game on a daily basis to maintain his **game point average** in the **game rankings**. Sometimes he takes **photographs** with his phone of particularly beautiful scenery or rock formations.

Joe now needs to replace the lost phone, but he only has limited funds to do so. Ideally he would like to remain on '**pay as you go**' to avoid being tied into paying monthly **contract fees**. He would like the new phone to have the same functionality as the old phone but preferably with a faster processor so that the 'kill the zombies' game can load faster. His wife may also use the new phone on occasions to make phone calls. He would use the new phone at least as much as he does now, possibly more if it has new functionality that he finds useful'.

The first thing to do with this information is to quickly go through it and highlight any nouns that you think might be relevant to the business area, i.e. in this case anything relevant to Joe's phone problem. If there are multiple occurrences of the same noun you only need to identify one of those occurrences, you don't need to highlight duplicates. You also don't need to highlight every noun, only the ones that are relevant, so nouns such as 'rock', 'expedition', 'pocket' etc. are not highlighted. 'Civil Engineer' is a job title and the job itself is not relevant to the issue so it hasn't been highlighted. However, it is useful to include any roles that are relevant. If there are nouns (concepts) that you are not sure about… which may or may not be relevant… include them anyway. Here we've included 'game point average' and 'game rankings' as potential concepts, mainly because the concept of 'game' is most likely within the business domain. Are these really concepts, or are they merely attributes, properties, of another concept? With every step in this approach you will need to do some iterative analysis, so defining what is a relevant concept and what is an attribute (or property) of a concept will need to be carried out as part of the analysis.

You also need to go through the 'As Is' process diagram and the list of problem statements and identify any other potential concepts. Make sure you go through all the notes that have been recorded against the processes as well. From the Joe Bloggs example, there are four more concepts described in the process that could potentially be useful - 'phone box', 'home phone', 'phone user' and 'friend':

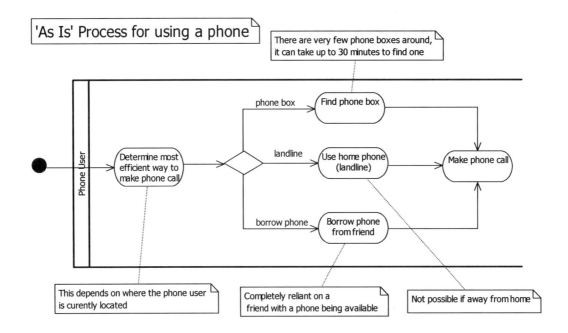

'As Is' Process for using a phone

There are very few phone boxes around, it can take up to 30 minutes to find one

Phone User

Determine most efficient way to make phone call

phone box → Find phone box

landline → Use home phone (landline)

borrow phone → Borrow phone from friend

Make phone call

This depends on where the phone user is curently located

Completely reliant on a friend with a phone being available

Not possible if away from home

There is also one additional concept from the problem statements -'camera' from the root cause analysis of problem 6:

6	Joe Bloggs can't take photographs of beautiful scenery or rock formations	Joe Bloggs has no access to a camera

Because this is an iterative approach, as you talk to the users in subsequent meetings and obtain further information on problems and process and requirements, you will be adding to, amending and refining the list of identified concepts, as well as working out how they relate to each other.

First though, let's put all these concepts we've initially identified into a diagram:

Fig. 15 – business concept diagram for the phone problem

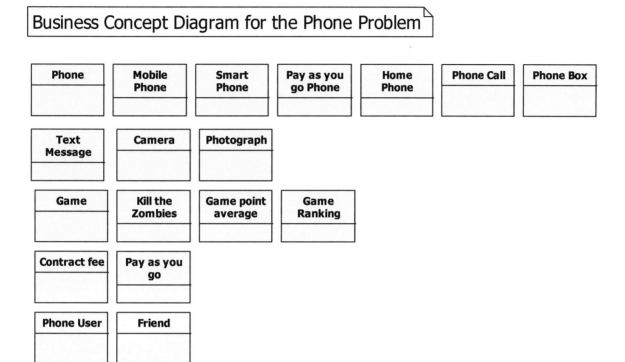

Okay, this looks pretty basic. We've grouped some of the concepts together, but that's about all. This gives us a very rough idea about the sort of information or things we're dealing with in relation to the overall problem, but apart from that it's not very helpful. We now need to start conducting some analysis on these concepts.

The first thing to do is to look for concepts that are 'types' of other concepts. So in this example we have a 'mobile' phone, a 'smart' phone, a 'pay as you go' phone and a 'home' phone, which are all types of phone. Let's start there and draw this relationship on the diagram:

Fig. 16 – generality relationships

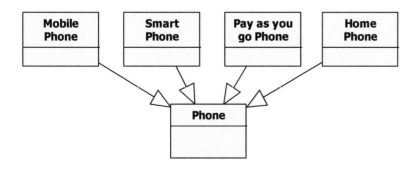

The line with a triangular arrow is standard UML (unified modelling language) notation meaning a 'generality'. A generality is a relationship between a particular object and a subtype of that object i.e. the line with an arrow means that any objects shown as pointing in the direction of the arrow to a particular object are subtypes of that object. This style of notation is also used for data architecture diagrams, so if you show this diagram to a data architect he/she should know exactly what it means.

We have another generality relationship that we can draw in the diagram – 'kill the zombies' is a type of game:

Fig. 17 – more generality relationships

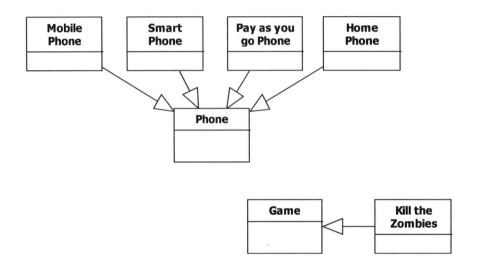

The next thing to do is to identify any other relationships between the concepts that we have identified. For example, what is the relationship between the concepts 'phone' and 'game'? Phone is a general concept, possibly too general for this particular problem. Remember, Joe Bloggs problem is really only concerned with his mobile phone. We've included the concept of home phone because the term cropped up in the 'As Is' process, but if we want to link 'game' to 'phone' we can't link them directly, as a home phone probably doesn't contain the functionality to play games. A mobile phone (at least one that Joe Bloggs would be interested in) does have this functionality though, as does a smart phone and probably a 'pay as you go' phone. So with a bit of analysis, we could state that both a 'smart phone' and a 'pay as you go' phone are types of 'mobile phone' and we can link 'Game' to 'Mobile Phone'. Are the concepts 'Phone' and 'Home Phone' even relevant to the problem? We can probably state up front that they are not in scope… the issue is around Joe Bloggs mobile phone, not his home phone or a phone in general. So we could take those concepts out of the diagram altogether. However unless we are 100% sure, this would be an assumption (rule number 2 – beware of assumptions!). Remember that you may not know what concepts are going to be in or out of scope at this early stage in the process… if there is any sense of doubt in your mind, keep the concepts in the diagram!

For now, we will keep these two concepts in the diagram:

Fig.18 – Addition of an association relationship

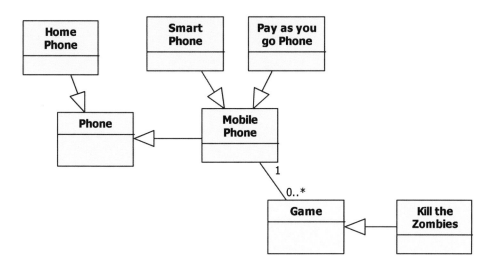

We have connected the concepts 'Game' and 'Mobile Phone' using a single line. In UML notation, this is called an association and does exactly what it says… it describes an association or relationship between two objects. You could state exactly what kind of an association the line is describing… for example you could add some text on the line itself to describe the relationship e.g. by adding the word 'contains' or the words 'can contain' to the line you are indicating that a mobile phone can contain games. However, which way do you read the text? If you read it from the game to the mobile phone it doesn't make sense. I don't normally add text descriptions to these lines… it can actually cause confusion when reading the diagram.

You will also notice that there are some numbers positioned at each end of the association. These numbers indicate 'multiplicity' – another UML term. Multiplicity states how many of one object can be associated with the other object. In this example, we are saying that one mobile phone can be associated with zero or more games i.e. there may be zero or many games on a mobile phone. Multiplicity is very useful, because it can give us some nicely defined business rules.

Don't get too hung up on trying to make this diagram perfect. You are aiming to further establish an understanding of the work area… the primary goal of this diagram is to map out the terms used by the business and how you think they relate to one another. You are not trying to design a system database, nor are you trying to create something that has to be 100% accurate. We are still in the 'understanding' phase of the approach and this diagram is just another tool to aid in that understanding. Let's put some more detail into the diagram and carry on…

Fig. 19 – initial business concept diagram for the phone problem

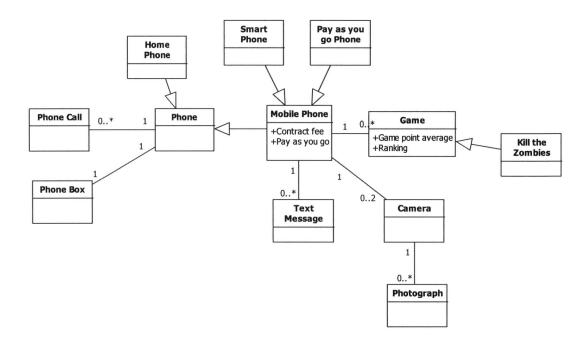

We have now added more association lines between concepts and included what we think are the correct multiplicities. If in doubt ask your users / subject matter experts… you can show them this diagram and because you are only using boxes, lines and arrows it should be simple enough to explain how to interpret the diagram. The users should be able to help with both the relationships between concepts and the multiplicity (business rules). We have also gone one step further in this diagram and added some attributes (properties) to a couple of the concepts. The game point average and game ranking were two concepts that were initially identified, but the question you need to ask yourself during the analysis of the concepts is… are these really concepts or are they properties of a concept? Again, don't get too hung up on this… it doesn't really matter if you have a concept called 'Game' connected to another concept called 'game point average', or if you've decided that 'game point average' is an attribute of a 'game'. You are not specifically trying to identify attributes at this stage… you are trying to identify concepts and use this information to clarify your understanding of the work area. If you have identified what you think are attributes of a concept you should add them to the diagram though, it will help later on during the requirements phase.

One more thing to note here… we have not put any roles on the diagram. In some circumstances it is very useful to show where roles fit in with the other concepts and in other circumstances it will just clutter the diagram. If you need to show that a particular role is an important concept, put it on the diagram. In this example there doesn't seem much point in putting 'friend' and 'phone user' on the diagram… it doesn't really add anything to our understanding of the business concepts in this situation. So we've left them out.

Creating a Glossary

Another good reason for defining the business concepts is to enable the creation of a glossary of terms. I cannot emphasize enough how important this is. Different people can use the same term with a completely different meaning applied to it, especially when you have groups of users working in different locations or even different departments. The users may be using several different terminologies to describe the same thing. Defining the business concepts gives you and the stakeholders the opportunity to come up with a common language – a means of communicating what is actually meant when they speak about a particular concept. Going back to the requirements specification template in chapter 3, you will notice there is a section there for a glossary. I would heavily advise using this to document a list of terms that are open to interpretation including any acronyms and synonyms that are used by the stakeholders. You can create a simple table showing the term and the definition of that term e.g.

Fig. 20 – a simple glossary table

Term	Definition
Game point average	The average number of points scored by a player in a game
Phone	Abbreviation of 'telephone' – a device used for communication

You can add examples if an example will help clarify the definition and you can group the terms by categorizing them e.g. by subject, by department, by process etc. Keep the table simple, and record the terms in the table in alphabetical order so that it is easy to find a particular term.

Concepts for the mathematical model problem

Let's take a quick look at what the business concept diagram for the mathematical model example might look like:

Fig. 21 – business concept diagram for the mathematical model problem

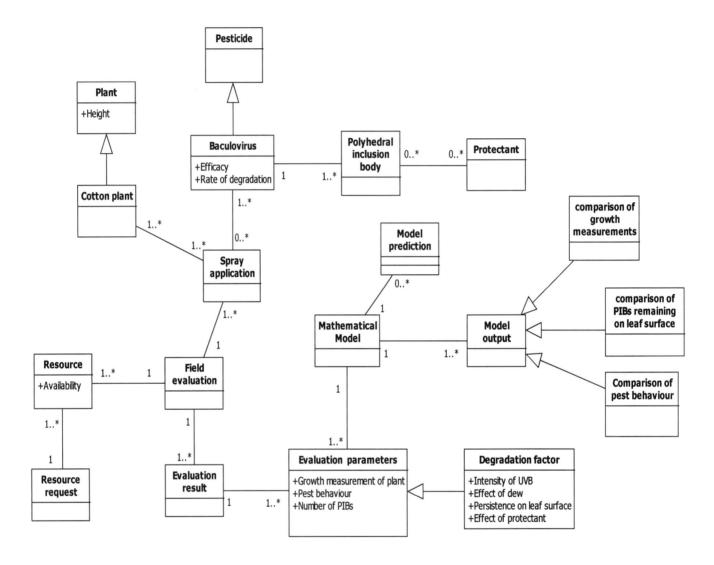

Looking at figure 21, we have applied exactly the same set of UML notation and analysis to the mathematical model problem as we did to the simple phone example. To get to the concepts, it is necessary to trawl through whatever documentation you have available – the background, the problem statements, the process diagrams and notes and identify what you think are the key business concepts. In this one diagram we are stating all of the following:

A baculovirus is a type of pesticide. A baculovirus is made up of one or more 'polyhedral inclusion bodies' (PIB's) which can be coated with zero or more protectants. One or more baculoviruses can be applied as a spray (perhaps multiple sprays) on one or more cotton plants. The spray application itself is applied in a field evaluation, where multiple sprays of baculovirus can be applied. A field evaluation requires one or more resources to carry out the evaluation. A resource has availability and one or more resources can be requested via a resource request. The field evaluation produces one or more evaluation results, which are based on one or more evaluation parameters. A degradation factor is a type of evaluation parameter, as is pest behavior, growth measurement of plant and number of PIBs. One or more evaluation parameters are used by the mathematical model. The model generates model predictions and produces model output. Model outputs include comparison of growth measurements, comparison of PIB's remaining on the leaf surface and comparison of pest behavior.

So the diagram itself is a pretty powerful tool for gaining a good understanding of what is happening, without having to write it all out in text. Again, don't worry too much about whether the diagram is 100% accurate. If a concept is really an attribute (or vice versa) or if there are multiplicity values missing… this is an iterative process and you will be returning to this diagram and amending it as you move towards defining the future state.

As for the glossary of terms, this needs to be agreed with the stakeholders. You can start by writing out your understanding of the term and then checking this with the stakeholders to ensure that the definition is correct. An agreed set of terminology complete with definitions is very useful for whatever project you are working on (see fig. 22 below for an example glossary):

Fig. 22 – glossary (incomplete) for the more complicated problem

Term	Definition
Baculovirus	A type of virus that occurs in certain species of insect
Degradation factor	A measure of how quickly something degrades when subject to certain conditions e.g. sunlight.
Efficacy	A measure of how effective something is
Evaluation parameter	Something that is measured or observed within a field evaluation
Field evaluation	An experiment involving the application of material to a plant or substrate under field conditions (as opposed to within a laboratory)
Mathematical Model	A model created to simulate certain conditions
Pest	An animal or insect that causes problems for people
Pest behavior	How a pest reacts when treated with a pesticide
Pesticide	A substance used to kill, repel or control pests
PIB	Polyhedral Inclusion Body. This is a polyhedral shaped wrapper / membrane that contains virions (viral DNA)
Protectant	A substance that provides protection for a pesticide against conditions that are likely to degrade that pesticide
Resource	A supply of people that can conduct field evaluations
Resource request	A request for resource
UVB	A particular wavelength of ultra violet radiation

Chapter 7 – Identify Competency Questions

Before we go any further, let's take another quick look at the diagram describing the approach:

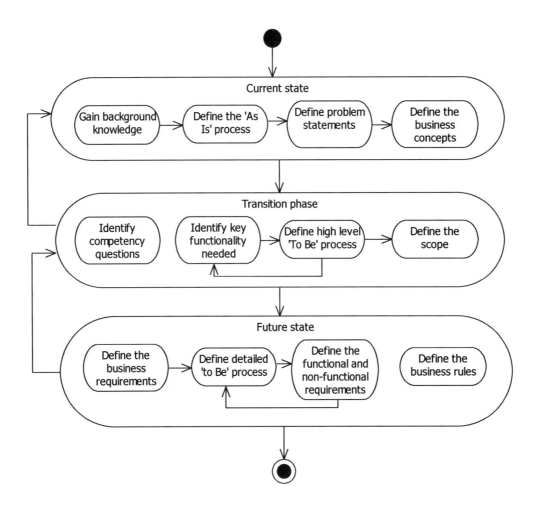

As you can see, we have now worked our way through the four activities that are necessary for gaining a good understanding of the current state and are now entering into the 'transition phase'. This does not mean that you are completely finished with the current state activities... you will find that both the problem statements and the business concept diagram in particular will need to be iteratively updated as you progress through the transition phase. You may also need to update the background with fresh information as it becomes available and even the 'as Is' process if something crucial has been missed. For now though, we are going to move on...

Many business analysts will have never heard of the 'competency question' technique. Until a couple of years ago, I had never heard about it either. I first heard about 'competency questions' while working on a project involving integrating data from a number of different data sources. The project involved taking data that was stored in different databases and combining the data to produce reports. Because the data was stored in data 'silo's' i.e. databases that were unconnected and did not communicate in any way with each other, it was necessary to create a 'data warehouse' type solution where the necessary data from each database was extracted and combined in the 'data warehouse'. From there, it was possible to search the combined data and generate reports.

To do this, a 'linked data' approach was used. 'Linked data' is basically a recommended best practice for exposing, sharing, and connecting pieces of data, information and knowledge on the Semantic Web (an extension of the web through defined standards that allows data to be readily shared and re-used). Instead of using relational databases with columns and rows of data such as you would find in an Oracle or SQL database, linked data uses the notion of linking data items using 'triples'. We will come on to 'triples' a bit later in this chapter, but for now all you need to know is that a 'triple' is a means of describing data in the form of a statement, which is: 'subject - 'predicate' - 'object'. These three entities form a 'triple' and an example of a triple would be 'Joe Bloggs (the subject) has (the predicate) a phone (the object)'.

A database containing triples is known as a triple store. There may be millions, perhaps billions of triples in a triple store. Where the real power of a triple store comes into effect is when the data statements (the triples) are linked to each other. By linking triples you can effectively create a huge web of information that can be queried. However, to create relationships between triples, you need to define each of the individual entities within each triple and map those entities to each other. And to do this, you need some form of 'semantic model', which describes the mapping of the entities to each other. And to create a semantic model, one of the best techniques for initially determining what information is relevant to the semantic model is the competency question technique...

What is a competency question?

Okay, I have now mentioned several (probably unfamiliar) terms including triples, triple stores, semantic models and mapping of entities, but what has all this jargon got to do with basic business analysis and the subject of this chapter... competency questions? What exactly is a 'competency question'? Let me explain. A 'competency question' is a query written in the form of a logic statement, based on a typical question that an expert might ask of a knowledge base.

In other words, a competency question is a logically phrased query, written in such a way that if you fed it as code into a computer, that computer should be able to generate an answer. It is written in such a way that 'things' (concepts) and properties of those 'things' (attributes) can be easily identified from the question. The term 'competency' means the ability to do something successfully or efficiently and that's exactly what we're trying to do here with competency questions... we want to be able to ask a question in a very efficient and successful manner in order to extract the maximum amount of relevant information out of the question. What distinguishes a 'competency question' from a normal, routine question is the fact that competency questions need to be structured in a very specific, logical way. They are written in a similar fashion to how a query (i.e. a database query) would be written. You can ask a fairly standard question such as 'where are my accounts stored?' or 'how many leaves are on a typical oak tree?' but these would not be competency questions. You can however, derive competency questions from these simple questions. Firstly, a competency question must be based around a 'concept' and its 'attributes', or in semantic terms, a 'thing' and its 'properties'. Secondly, a competency question is usually structured in one of two ways:

1. Show me one or more things that have these properties
2. Show me one or more properties for this thing

You should now be able to see that there is a strong relationship between the use of competency questions to identify things and properties, and the use of a business concept model to identify concepts and attributes. However there is one fundamental and very important difference. When we created our business concept diagram, we were identifying the concepts that were apparent through analysis of the current state situation. When we define competency questions we are effectively identifying concepts derived from questions that the users might want to ask of the solution i.e. the future state. And if your stakeholders are formulating questions regarding the future state, they are actually beginning to think about the type of information they will need in the future.

So although my introduction to competency questions was originally in relation to identifying the information needed to create a 'semantic model', I quickly realized that competency questions could also be used for helping stakeholders transition to thinking about the future state, as well as helping to define requirements around the querying and reporting of data.

Using competency questions for understanding data needs

Let's face it; if someone is inputting information into a software application, that person is probably going to want to access that information at some point. Why else is the information being recorded? The whole point of recording information is to make it available so that it can be used. Rather than ask your users about the information they would like to record, you should really be asking them about the information that they would like to use. Competency questions are a very useful means of determining what information is really needed by the stakeholders or in other words, what information people would like to search for and use.

By creating a list of competency questions, you are effectively asking the users to come up with a series of example queries that they would want to perform on the data. By doing this you are getting to the crux of what information the stakeholders really need and why they need it. Once you understand the sort of questions that will be asked of the information, you will be in a much better position to understand why a particular data field is needed.

Taking the question 'where are my accounts stored?' you could restructure this question into a proper competency question (formatted as a query) by some simple logical analysis.

'Show me all the data stores that contain accounts data for person (p)'.

In this example, the data store is a concept (thing) which will have several attributes (properties) such as 'location' and 'identifier'. 'Accounts data' is another concept that may have several attributes. We've also introduced a concept of a 'person' into this question and a 'person' can also be regarded as having attributes. The 'p' in brackets after 'person' indicates that this is an instance of a person; a named individual. The 'p' represents any named individual person.

For the question 'how many leaves on a typical oak tree?' we can translate this into the following competency question:

'Show me the total number of leaves for oak tree (x) where oak tree (x) represents a typical oak tree'. In this case we are looking for a quantifiable number of leaves that belong to a representative oak tree. 'Number of leaves' can be regarded as an attribute of a tree (the concept). The tree can be regarded as being of type 'oak', so 'type of tree' might be another attribute.

Another example:

'I want to know the names of all the people living in the UK whose birthday falls on 17th May'. This is already worded in something close to a competency question format, but if you want to be even more specific and logical you could reword this slightly e.g.:

'Show me the names of all people living in the UK where birth date equals 17th May.'

The birth date is an attribute of a person and a person is the concept.

The best way of defining competency questions is actually to start with a basic 'standard' question and work out what the competency question is afterwards. Once you have analyzed the original question and rephrased it so that it reads like a query, you should then be able to identify the concepts and attributes that would be required to answer that query. This can sometimes be difficult to do as some of the concepts (and attributes) may have to be derived logically. However, we will run through some examples and explain the thinking behind this.

We will start by taking a quick look at some theoretical questions based around the example of the Joe Bloggs phone problem. It is much easier to document competency questions in a tabular format in order to see the original questions, the refined competency questions and any concepts and attributes that have been identified and derived from the competency questions. The table below shows an example of how you might structure this information in a tabular format. Make sure that you list clearly any identified attributes against the relevant concept:

Fig. 23 – table showing list of competency questions for the phone example:

Question	Competency question	Concepts	Attributes
1. How much credit have I got remaining on my phone?	Show me the amount of credit remaining on phone (p)	Credit Phone	Amount remaining Model, ID
2. What's my high score in 'kill the zombies' game?	Show me the high score for person (p) for game (g)	Person Game	name High score, name
3. What's my game point average for 'kill the zombies'?	Show me the game point average for person (p) for game (g)	Person Game	name Game point average, name
4. How many phone calls did I make last month?	Show me total number of phone calls made for all dates within month (m)	Phone call Month	Quantity, Date Name
5. How much space (for photos) have I got left on my phone?	Show me total amount of storage capacity remaining on phone (p)	Storage capacity Phone	Amount remaining Model, ID

Okay, let's go through these questions one by one…

Question 1: By asking how much credit there is remaining on the phone, we are asking for an amount remaining. 'Credit' is a concept which probably has one or more attributes e.g. total amount, amount remaining etc. In this case we have identified the attribute 'amount remaining' from this question. We also have a concept of a 'phone' and we have added (p) against this concept when restructuring the question. The reason why we've added (p) against the concept is to show that this is an instance of the concept, just as we put an (x) against the oak tree concept in the example above… to show that we're talking about a particular instance of the concept. So in this question we are talking specifically about a particular phone and we are calling it phone (p). You can use any letter you like to show the instance of a concept, it doesn't matter. If you didn't show that this was a particular instance of a phone then the question changes emphasis completely… it becomes 'show me the amount of credit remaining on a phone'. This is a very different question and is no longer a logical and easy question to answer. Which phone are we talking about? How are we going to answer this question?

Question 2: There is a particular instance of a person (p) implied in this question with the use of the word 'my' which is probably going to be Joe Bloggs in this case. However, there is a possibility that it may not be Joe Bloggs as the high score relates to the game. By using (p) to represent the instance of a person it is possible for Joe to view high scores of other people as well if he wants to. We have used game (g) to represent the instance of a particular game, but we could have used game (kill the zombies) if we are absolutely sure that this is the only game that Joe is going to be playing. Better to err on the side of caution when you specify an instance of a thing though and give it a generic identifier, just in case!

Question 3 is virtually the same as question 2, with a different property being asked for.

Question 4: Here we are asking for one or more things (phone calls) with a date property. In terms of restructuring this into a competency question, we need to identify what the properties of the thing are, so that the question can be answered logically. The output of a competency question is always going to be in terms of properties and one or more values of those properties. By asking the question 'how many', we are effectively asking for an amount (or quantity) of that thing. In this case, we are talking about number of phone calls, so we need to know the number (quantity) of phone calls made. Because the number of calls occurs over a set time, we also need to have a date property. Because the output is for a specific month we also need to know which month, so there must be a property identifying which month of the year we are interested in.

Question 5: The original question was phrased quite casually with the word 'space', but we can make this more precise by using the term 'storage capacity' to represent 'space', 'memory', 'room' etc. 'Storage capacity remaining' is a quantifiable property of storage capacity, probably measured in megabytes or gigabytes.

Categorizing the competency questions

For the table in fig. 23 we created four columns to describe the original question, the refined question, a list of identified concepts for each question and a list of identified properties for each concept. However, the users may provide you with a large number of questions on a range of different subjects. The questions may also be related to specific parts of their process. If you have a significant number of questions (more than 10) that can be categorized by subject matter, work area, organization, process etc. I would recommend that you create another column in your table to show the categorization of the questions. This will make your list of competency questions much easier to refer back to, especially in cases where you might want to find all the questions related to a particular categorization.

If we were to obtain a list of competency questions for the more complicated example based on the mathematical model, we would probably want to group the questions by subject matter or process due to the potentially large number of questions that might be asked. To show this, I have made up a few competency questions that the users might potentially want to ask and documented these hypothetical questions in fig 24:

Fig. 24 – example table including an additional column for categorizing questions:

Category	Question	Competency question	Concepts	Attributes
Requests	Which requests are awaiting approval?	Show me all requests where approval status is not equal to 'approved'	Request	Approval status
Resource	Is there any resource available to carry out this field evaluation?	Show me all resource of status (available) for conducting field evaluation (f)	Resource Field evaluation	Resource amount, Resource status Field Evaluation ID
Evaluation Results	What is the average plant height measured in the field during the 3rd quarter of 2015?	Show me the average height of plant (p) for all field evaluations carried out in months (July, August, September) for year (2015)	Plant Field evaluation	Height, Average height, Height measurement date Field Evaluation ID
Model output	How does plant height measurement taken in the field for 20 plants compare with that predicted by the model on a month by month basis?	For each month, show me the average height of plant group (g) for all field evaluations compared with the average height of plant group (g) predicted by the model	Plant Group Field evaluation	Plant Group ID, Number of plants, Average height, Height measurement date, Predicted average height Field Evaluation ID

Apart from the additional column though, there would be no difference when applying the competency question technique to a very complicated problem as opposed to the simple example we have just worked through, except for the fact that you would have a lot more competency questions and you stand a good chance of identifying a lot more concepts and attributes!

So assuming that you now have a list of competency questions and their related concepts and attributes, what are you going to do with them? Well, we could stop right here if all you are interested in is identifying a set of typical queries and a list of concepts and attributes needed in order to support a query and reporting project. If you are using this technique to help with a query and reporting project, the competency questions will complement the concept diagram and act as an additional check for the concepts and attributes you have already defined, as well as provide a valuable insight into the sort of queries that the stakeholders are likely to be interested in. However, if the purpose of defining competency questions is for a project that involves linking data, there is one more step you might want to take to help with this – creating a semantic data model.

Creating a Semantic model

I mentioned the term 'semantic model' earlier in this chapter. A 'semantic model' is a type of data model which consists of a network of concepts and the relationships between those concepts. The concepts and the relationships between those concepts are often referred to as an 'ontology' or in other words, a semantic model that describes 'knowledge'.

If you want more comprehensive knowledge about semantic modeling, rdf (resource description framework), URI's (Uniform Resource Identifiers) and the use of models for creating ontologies, I would suggest looking elsewhere as there is enough material that could be written on these subjects to fill another book twice over. A good reference book to explain these terms properly would be 'Semantic Web for the Working Ontologist - Effective Modeling in RDFS and OWL' by Dean Allemang and James Hendler.

I just want to give a very brief overview about how to create a semantic model in this chapter, not go into any details on rdf, URI's, ontology's or the correct way to structure triples. So what you have here is a very brief description of how to create a simple semantic model – just enough detail for you as a business analyst to be able to create one of these models for use in a linked data (data integration) project and hand it over to a development team or Ontologist, for use as the basis for further work.

A semantic model does have similarities to a business concept model. The main difference is in the drawing of the relationships between the concepts and the attributes. A business concept model as described in chapter 6 deals solely with concepts and the attributes belonging to those concepts. The relationships in a business concept diagram are drawn as associations between concepts in a very object oriented way – we have two objects and there is some sort of an association between these two objects. The objects have attributes. End of story. With a semantic model, the diagram is more focused on looking at a series of statements or facts about the concepts and their attributes. A semantic model shows the relationship between concepts and attributes as a three part relationship… the concept (thing), the relationship itself, and the object of that relationship, which could either be an attribute (property) of that thing, a literal value, or maybe another 'thing'. This three part relationship is known as a 'triple'. The three parts that make up a triple are known as a subject (the thing of interest) an object (the thing or literal value that the subject is concerned with) and a predicate (the relationship between the subject and the object).

Here is a very simple example of a triple:

Joe Bloggs has a phone

Joe Bloggs is the subject. 'Has' is the predicate, the relationship. Phone is the object… it's what Joe Bloggs has.

We can draw this in semantic model form like this:

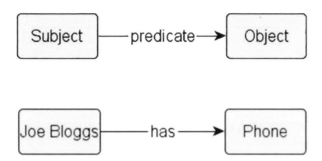

Let's quickly take another look at the competency questions in fig. 23 for the phone example and see how these can be translated into a semantic model. The first competency question - *Show me the amount of credit remaining on phone (p)* has given us the concepts of 'credit' and 'phone'. Credit has an attribute – 'amount remaining'. Phone has an identifier and is of a particular model. So expressing this information in the form of triples will give us something like:

Fig. 25 – example semantic model:

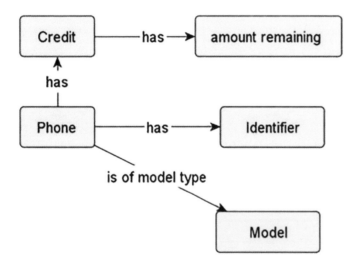

If we know that the phone's identifier was a particular serial number e.g. JB123456 and that the model of phone was a Nokia, we could show this as follows:

Fig. 26 – example semantic model showing objects as literals

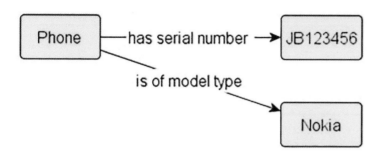

As a piece of data, each part of the triple would have a unique identifier known as a 'uniform resource identifier' or URI. This identifier enables a differentiation to be made between two concepts that might look identical but actually have different meanings. An example of this would be the word 'turkey', which might refer to a bird or a country. Turkey the bird would have a different URI to Turkey the country.

You can quickly surmise that if we were to create a triple for every possible combination of information that needs to be recorded within a work area we are going to end up with thousands, possibly millions or even billions of triples (and URI's). And that is absolutely fine; that is exactly what we would expect! The whole purpose of viewing the data in this way, as triples which all link together to form a gigantic web or network of related information, is to facilitate searching for information. A computer, when tasked with a particular query such as 'show me the amount of credit remaining on phone (JB123456)' can quickly trawl through these triples and locate the answer. Of course the speed of the search will depend on the processor speed of the computer, but the key thing here is that it doesn't matter if the data itself is located in multiple different databases or a single database.

For the example shown in fig. 25 we may be searching for data across several databases. The amount of credit remaining may be held in a database belonging to the network provider. The make and model of the phone may be held in a database belonging to the phone manufacturing company. Our unique instance of 'Joe Bloggs' may be held in a database belonging to the tax office. If this information was available as triples then 'Joe Bloggs' would have a unique identifier (URI) that could be referenced by the other databases. So instead of recreating (and thereby duplicating) the name 'Joe Bloggs' in the phone manufacturing company database and the network provider database, you could reference Joe Bloggs from the tax office database and a search could pull up the name 'Joe Bloggs', the make of phone he owned and the amount of credit remaining on that phone without having to duplicate this information in each database.

Basically, if you want to integrate or link data from various different data sources and pull it together to create an output, using triples is a very effective way of doing this. And it reduces or even eliminates the need to hold duplicated data in several different databases.

An example semantic model

Let's go back to our semantic model and the competency questions. Using just the concepts and attributes that we have identified in fig. 23 for the phone example, we might end up with a model that looks something like this:

Fig. 27 – Example semantic model for the phone example

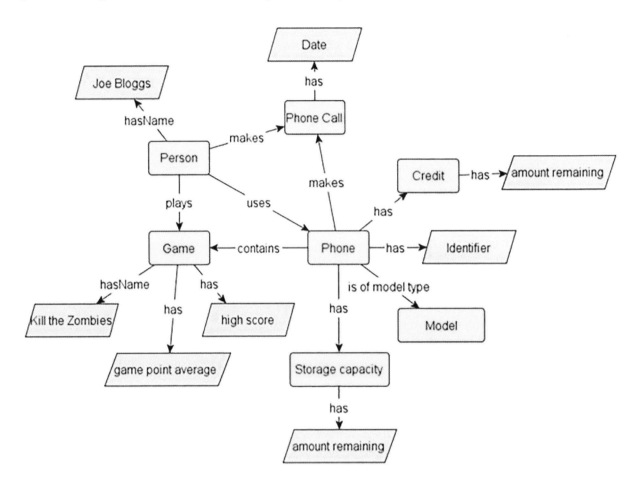

I would recommend you use color coding as in the above example to distinguish between what you think are the key concepts (the yellow boxes) and what you think are attributes of those concepts (the green boxes). Using this color coding makes the diagram easier to read as well as imparting more information to whoever needs to use this diagram (probably the development team including an Ontologist). This is not a UML (unified modeling language) diagram so you may find that a dedicated UML diagramming tool is not capable of producing this kind of diagram. However, you could use Microsoft Visio or PowerPoint or any tool with a suitable template that will allow you to draw this type of diagram.

The diagram itself shows a particular interpretation of the information that we know is going to be queried by the stakeholders. The information is displayed in the form of a series of linked triples, each triple representing a particular fact. A game has a high score. A game has a name – 'kill the zombies' in this case. A phone has storage capacity etc. You can take this diagram and explain it to the development team responsible for creating a linked data solution and they can use it as the basis for a design.

If you want a little challenge, try drawing up a semantic model for the more complicated example based on the mathematical model, using just the information from the competency questions in fig. 24. Remember though, just as with the concept diagram in chapter 6, you don't need to spend hours trying to get this model absolutely correct. You are not trying to create a definitive design here; you are providing information that will be useful for the development team, who are themselves responsible for the creation of a design. Good luck!

Chapter 8 – Identify Key Functionality Needed

In this chapter, we are going to use the knowledge gained from describing the 'As Is' process and the business concepts to begin the transition towards the 'To Be' process and the requirements for the future. Identifying the functionality required is one of the most important steps in working towards a solution; it helps bridge that tricky gap between what the stakeholders currently do and what they want to do in the future.

Assuming you've already created an 'As Is' process diagram, this next step is going to be relatively simple. However, if what you are working on is basically a new idea, a clean slate with no prior process in place, things become a little trickier. We will discuss how to deal with this type of scenario later on, but first let's go back to our original examples and take a look at the more complicated example of the mathematical model first. The 'As Is' process for the more complicated problem of the mathematical model is described in chapter 4 and redrawn below:

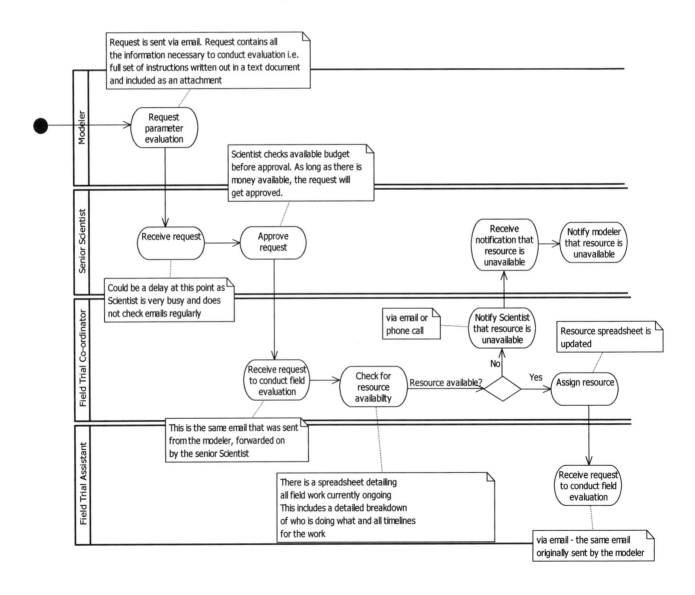

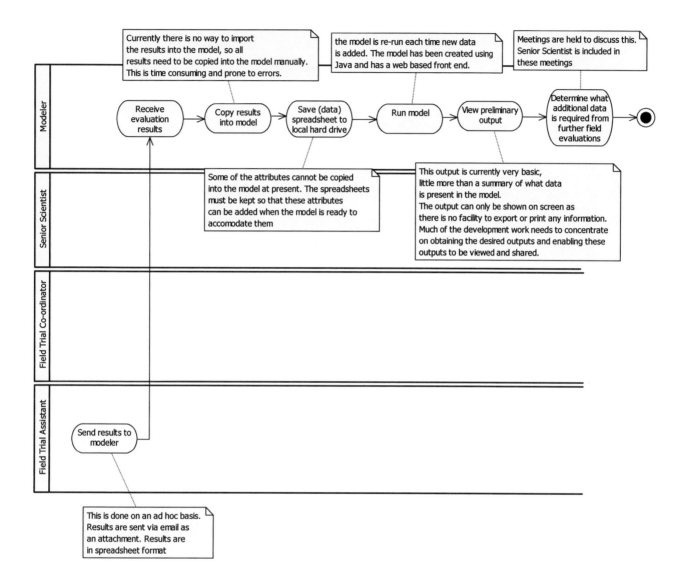

Because we only diagrammed the beginning and the end of the process, we have probably missed some process steps that may have occurred in the middle, but let's not worry about those for the moment. These two diagrams describe most of the process for the mathematical model example including the identification of four roles that are involved in the process: a modeler, a senior scientist, a field trial co-ordinator and a field trial assistant. We will need to do a little analysis work to transition from describing the 'as is' process steps to defining the functionality required, but it's not going to be too difficult because we are going to be using two specific techniques to help us. The first technique is the creation of a 'use case' diagram.

Use Cases

I have always thought that the term 'use case' is quite a strange term... it was created by Ivor Jacobson back in 1992 and is meant to describe 'a sequence of actions that an actor performs (usually within a system) to achieve a particular goal'. In UML (unified modeling language) terminology, roles are known as actors. There have been many books written about use cases and how to use them for requirements gathering. Two books that you might find useful if you want to find out more about use cases are:

Writing Effective Use Cases by Alistair Cockburn

The Art of Writing Use Cases by Rebecca Wirfs-Brock

Some of the books written about use cases and how to describe them range from the fairly simple to the overly complicated. A use case written as text can have 'pre-conditions' and 'post-conditions'. It can be a 'business level' or 'system level' use case. It can have 'alternate paths' and 'secondary scenario's'. A textual use case can be 'casual' or 'fully dressed'. I am not going to explain these terminologies here, but if you follow some of the methodologies for writing use cases as formal documents you will probably be spending some significant time on the project writing and refining them. Feel free to check out the books to understand more about use case and these terms, but do not worry too much about the detail.

I do not recommend that you write textual use cases as described in these books, mainly because it takes an inordinate amount of time to do so. The other reason I do not recommend the formal use case approach is because many users have a hard time reviewing the text. A single 'fully dressed' use case containing several 'alternate paths' and/or different scenarios can run to several pages. For a large project you may need to describe in excess of 50 or even 100 use cases. You can easily end up with two or even three hundred pages of use case text. Many stakeholders just don't have the patience to review and agree so much text. And more than likely you won't have the time to write and correct them either.

For this approach I would suggest that you think of a use case not as a textual use case *per se*, but as a piece of functionality that is required by a user. This piece of functionality is something the user wants to do when interacting with the solution. Each piece of functionality can be described by a series of steps or activities that occur when interacting with the solution. We will use a UML use case diagram to describe these pieces of functionality and the 'sequence of actions' definition still applies. However, there is no need to get hung up on the differences between a 'business use case and a 'system' use case, nor is there any reason to try to document pre-conditions and post-conditions and alternate paths…. Let's just stick to the basics.

Take a look at the following diagram:

Fig. 28 – Example use case diagram:

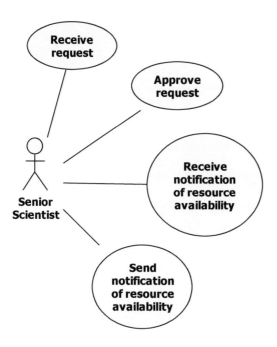

For this diagram we have taken the role 'Senior Scientist' identified from the 'As Is' process and associated that role with four things that the Senior Scientist currently does. We have changed the wording slightly for the two processes that deal with resource availability but basically all we've done is transpose the processes from the 'As Is' process diagram into a use case diagram. Note that the use cases (functionalities) are written in the format: verb – noun. Try to keep to this verb – noun format when drawing up use cases. You should start seeing a pattern emerging, and this pattern is what we're going to use for our second technique.

Use Case (functionality) patterns

Remember all of the work that we've done on concepts in the last couple of chapters? This is where some of that work comes into play. In the above diagram (fig. 28) we have two concepts... 'Request' and 'Resource'. Thinking logically and in terms of functionality when interacting with a solution, there is only a limited number of things that can be done with or to a particular concept. Of course, the things that can be done with a concept are very much dependent on the concept itself, but generally speaking there is a limit to how a user can interact with a particular thing (concept). In general, you can create something. You can change it (update or amend). You can destroy or remove it (delete). You might be able to send or receive it. In fact, although the list of possible options is very much dependent on the concept, it's actually not that vast a list. Some of the most common (generic) ones can be seen in the following table:

Fig. 29 – Generic list of things you can commonly do to a concept in terms of functionality:

Most commonly used:	Examples
Create (or define)	Create request
Generate	Generate report
Record	Record project details
Update (or edit or amend)	Update project details
View (or visualize)	View request
Send	Send notification
Receive	Receive notification
Approve	Approve request
Delete (or archive)	Delete project
Review (or check)	Review project report
Conduct (carry out)	Conduct field evaluation
Analyze (or calculate)	Analyze results
Assign	Assign work
Search (or query)	Search results data
Store (or archive)	Store results data
Import	Import data
Export	Export data
Purchase	Purchase stock
Sell	Sell stock

Of course it is easily possible to come up with a lot more, especially if you are dealing with something a little out of the ordinary. However, the above list of verbs although by no means comprehensive, is a good starting point for a 'pattern' that can be shared with the users. You should be able to come up with your own list of commonly used verbs if the ones listed above are insufficient for your particular work area.

What do I mean by using this list of verbs as a pattern? Well, I'm basically using these commonly used verbs as a re-usable check list with the users. We have identified a list of concepts that are relevant and you as the analyst can now ask questions about these concepts based on the list of commonly used verbs.

To do this, you will need to use the 'As Is' process as a starting point. Begin by working through each of the 'as is' process steps with the users. For each process step, ask the users to think about what else they would like to do in terms of functionality. If there are problems documented for the process step, ask them what functionality they would require in order to address the problems. Don't go into solution - concentrate solely on the 'what'. Ask them about what they would need to do in the future with any concepts that appear in the process step, including any concepts that appear in the notations. Don't go into too much detail - you are only looking for functionality at this stage.

Think also about the overall objectives for this piece of work. If necessary, talk to the users again about the objectives - what exactly do they want and why do they want it? What functionality will they need to meet these objectives?

Let's take an example from the 'As Is' process diagram for the mathematical model:

Fig. 30 – Example 'As Is' process steps:

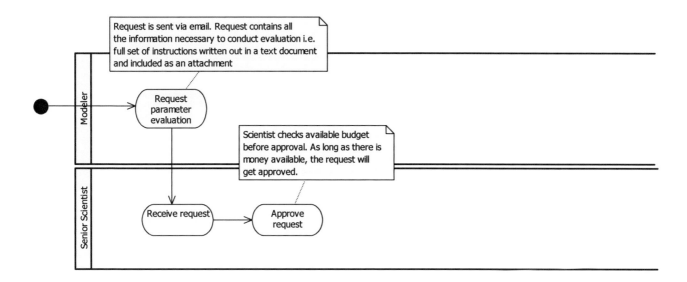

The first process step is 'request parameter evaluation', carried out by a modeler. What would be needed to describe this process step in terms of functionality? 'Request parameter evaluation' is effectively describing the process for submitting a request. To submit a request, there are several things that the modeler will need to do in terms of functionality. The modeler will want to **create** the request, maybe have the ability to **update** the request, and also to **send** the request to the senior scientist. Don't worry about 'how' this is done... we now have three distinct pieces of functionality that the modeler needs to be able to do. Go on to the next process step - 'receive request' carried out by the senior scientist. Anything else needed here in terms of functionality before the approval step? Nothing obvious, but moving on to the approval step there is a note stating that the budget needs to be checked before approval. This is another piece of functionality that will be required then... the ability to check the budget. Keep going.... every time you come across a potential piece of functionality that could be required, document it as a use case in a use case diagram and associate the functionality with the responsible role.

You will also need to carry out some analysis on these use cases as you go. Try to stay at the same level of detail as used in the 'as is' process diagram. Generally, you should find that you can equate a single use case to a single process step. However, where you have a process step that is a little vague or open to interpretation as to what exactly would be required, you might need to break it down into more detail to describe the functionality behind the process, just as we did above for the 'request parameter evaluation'. We broke this process step down into three distinct pieces of functionality so that later on we would be able to describe the series of actions that need to occur when creating the request, when updating the request and when sending the request. If a developer was to build this piece of functionality in a system, a single use case called 'request parameter evaluation' may not be detailed enough to describe the functionality required.

When running through your checklist of verbs that might be applied against a particular concept you don't have to confine yourself solely to this list. You can also use brainstorming techniques with the users to determine if there is anything else (in terms of functionality) the user wants to do.

An example use case diagram

Let's use the mathematical model example and take a look at an example use case diagram describing the functionality that a modeler would potentially like to have in the future. To get to this point, you will need to have reviewed the 'As Is' process diagrams in fig. 8 and fig. 9 with the users and identified the key functionality that is currently being used. You will also need to have asked questions about each process step in order to determine if extra functionality is required. You will have specifically identified any extra functionality needed to address problems and to meet objectives:

Fig. 31 – Use case diagram showing potential functionalities required in the future by a modeler:

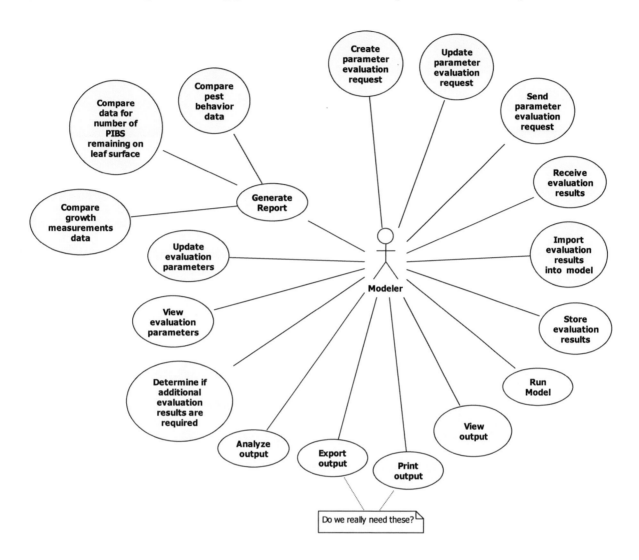

When creating these diagrams, try to draw the use cases in the order that they will be performed, from top to bottom in a clockwise fashion. By doing this, you will be making life a little easier for yourself when it comes to using the diagrams later on for helping define the 'To Be' process.

We are going to go through the diagram in fig. 31 in a little more detail now in order to explain how these functionalities have been identified from the 'As Is' process diagram. So let's take a step back in time, to the point where you are meeting with the users and you have the 'As Is' process diagram displayed so that everyone can see it. The first thing to do is to create a use case diagram with your UML tool and add the first role that appears in the process diagram into your use case diagram. Make sure that you show the users exactly what you are doing, so that they can comment and contribute as necessary. Go through each step in the process diagram for that role with the users and identify the functionality required for the process step. Add the functionality to the use case diagram as a use case and draw an association line between the role and the use case. Keep going... repeat for each role.

For the example use case diagram in fig. 31 we have concentrated on the modeler role. Looking at the use cases in order from top left clockwise, we have broken the first process (request parameter evaluation) into three use cases, as explained earlier. Later on we may find that we don't actually need all three use cases, but we will discuss this in another chapter. The rest of the process steps that a modeler performs appear in the diagram described in fig. 9 which is reproduced below for convenience:

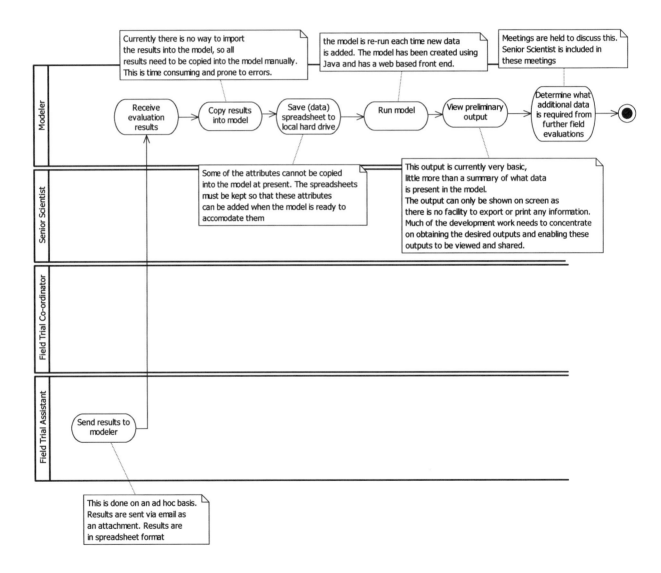

The first step that the modeler carries out in the above 'As Is' process is to receive evaluation results. The modeler still needs to be able to do this in the future. We can keep the wording of the use case the same as the wording in the process step because the ability to receive something is a discrete piece of functionality. We also have the verb 'receive' listed as one of our key re-usable verbs.

The next process step, is called 'copy results into model'. We know from the note that this step is a problem - it is carried out manually, it takes time and there is the potential for errors to occur. Ideally, the modeler would like to import the results directly into the model. So in the use case diagram, we have a use case called 'import evaluation results into model'.

What else would the modeler like to do with the evaluation results? The As Is' process step reads 'save spreadsheet to local hard drive'. However, if we are going to import the results directly into the model then they may not actually be in the form of a spreadsheet. A local hard drive may no longer be the preferred option for storage. The functionality required here is to store the results, irrespective of solution. 'Store' is another key verb from our patterns table so we will call this use case 'Store evaluation results'.

Moving on, the next step in the process is to run the model. We have kept the wording of the use case the same as the process step. After the model has been run, the modeler wants to 'view preliminary output'. According to the note attached to this step, there are some significant issues with this part of the process. What functionality do we need here to be able to address these issues? There is mention of being able to export and share the output and of being able to print the output. There is mention that the output is only able to be viewed in a simplistic form currently.

We will need to explore the functionality required here in more detail. Who else needs to view the output? Does it really need to be exported to somewhere else or should it just be made available so that others can see it? Who else would need access permissions to see it? Why does it need to be printed? By asking questions about the actual functionality required here, you are starting to delve into the requirements and get the users thinking more in terms of the future.

There is obviously additional functionality required here, but it may not be possible to identify exactly what it is that is really needed... at least not yet. If you come across a situation like this where certain functionality may or may not be required but there is uncertainty as to what is really needed, you have two choices:

1. Document all the potential functionality anyway. In this case, we would create additional use cases for 'export output', 'print output' and any other pieces of functionality that might be identified during discussion with the users.

2. Keep it simple. Stick with a single use case - 'view output' and explore the complexity later, when you start defining the 'To Be' process.

Personally I prefer to keep things simple. However, because this is an area of potential complexity I have added 'export output' and 'print output' to the use case diagram. We will need to revisit the use cases anyway when defining the 'To Be' process, so to avoid becoming bogged down in a discussion where things are ambiguous, make a note that there is more work to be done in this area. Capture exactly what the user thinks they want to do and move on. If you do decide to create use cases as place holders for later discussion, make sure you identify them as such e.g. with a note against the use case(s) in question.

During your discussions with the users, you may identify process steps that are missing from the 'As Is' diagram. We have a use case called 'analyze output' in the use case diagram that does not correspond with any process step because it was missed during the original documentation of the 'As Is' process. If this occurs, the easiest thing to do is to just add the missing process step into the 'As Is' diagram for completeness. You also need to keep your concept diagrams updated... any new concepts (or changes to existing concepts) coming out of this exercise need to be added to the concept diagram. The glossary should also be updated if required.

'Determine if additional evaluation results are required' is the final step in the 'As Is ' process diagram. This determination may or may not represent a discrete piece of functionality. We are not sure... it may be something that occurs as part of the analysis as opposed to a piece of functionality in itself. Again, you will need to decide whether to add it as a use case or to explore the functionality required in more detail during the 'To Be' process definition. In this case, we have added it to the use case diagram with the understanding that we can delete it if it turns out not to be needed as a discrete piece of functionality.

Going back now to the use case diagram (fig.31), the two use cases for viewing and updating evaluation parameters have been added as these were identified as additional functionality that the modeler would like to have. Finally, we have a generic use case called 'Generate report' with three other use cases representing the types of report required associated with the 'Generate report' use case. Now, in UML there are two other types of association that can be used in a use case diagram for linking one use case to another: 'extend' and 'include'. Extend usually means that a use case is an optional piece of functionality that is an extension of the main use case. However, it can also mean that the extended use case represents an alternate path. Include usually means that the functionality described in a use case is included in another use case. It can also represent re-use, where specific functionality described in one use case can be included (or re-used) in another use case.

To keep things simple with your stakeholders and to avoid over-complicating the diagram, I would recommend that you do not use these two association types. If you need to associate one use case with another as we have done with 'generate report' and the associated use cases, just use a simple association line. This will save you time trying to explain to the stakeholders what 'extend' and 'include' means!

The 'new idea' scenario

I mentioned earlier in this chapter that we would come back to the scenario where you don't have an 'As Is' process already defined. In fact, you may not have anything at all defined up front... just an idea. In this situation, working with your stakeholders to create a use case diagram to explore the new idea can be an incredibly powerful tool... in fact it can be just as powerful as using a brainstorming technique.

Imagine the scene... you are sitting in a room with five stakeholders and they say to you... "We have an idea. We don't currently do this at the moment and we're not sure exactly what we want, but we would like to do something based around kinetic energy". Okay, that is a pretty vague starting point and you could use a brainstorming session to try to flesh out what it is they want to do with 'kinetic energy'. Brainstorming is a very useful technique but unless you focus the session you tend to end up with lots of 'stuff', some of which is useful, some not so useful, and all at various levels of detail. Creating a use case diagram as a means of fleshing out a new idea focuses the stakeholders and helps in defining the functionality required for this new idea.

Start with the roles... who will be involved with this kinetic energy idea? Who is it for? A Scientist? An energy consultant? A consumer? A person who eats fish? Whatever... just like a brainstorming session you will need to capture the output, but instead of using flipcharts or sticky notes and lots of text, create a use case diagram with actors. Look at each actor and ask the question, what do you think this role needs to do regarding kinetic energy? Because 'kinetic energy' is a concept, you can use your functionality patterns to help define what it is they want to do with this concept. Do they want to generate it? Export it? Purchase it? Record information about it? How do they want to work with it? What other concepts come into play when you talk to your stakeholders about 'kinetic energy'? What do they want to do with these other concepts? By asking a series of questions focused on the role and the functionality you can quickly build up a picture describing the new idea; a picture in the form of a use case diagram:

Fig. 32 – Example use case diagram created from a discussion exploring a new idea:

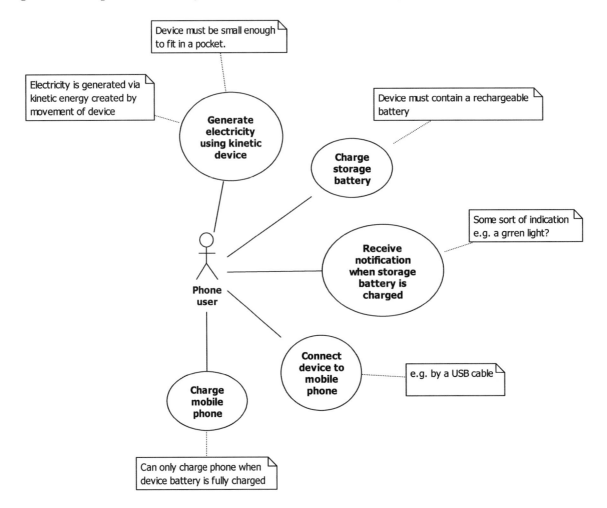

Fig. 32 represents a very simple use case diagram showing one potential use for 'kinetic energy'. Notes have been used to capture more detail including some requirements. It does not matter if the idea is as high level and vague as 'something to do with kinetic energy' or as detailed and focused as 'we want a new tool that can automatically calculate the distance between any two points based on their GPS (global positioning system) co-ordinates.' The questions you ask about the roles and functionalities will still be the same. Just focus on the 'things', the concepts that become apparent during the discussion, for example 'geographical location', 'GPS co-ordinate' etc. and the functionality pattern that might apply to those concepts (view, record, calculate etc.). The combination of the concepts that are relevant and the functionality (what people want to do with those concepts) will enable you to create a use case diagram with the stakeholders, which can then be used to explore the new idea.

Chapter 9 – Define the High Level 'To Be' Process

You have probably spent several hours so far doing all of the groundwork; defining the background, the 'as is' process, the problem statements, concepts, competency questions and functionalities. All of this effort up front makes the rest of the approach both easier and quicker to complete. Each progressive step we have taken so far has built on the previous steps. Likewise, the functionalities that we have just defined are going to come in very useful for helping to define the 'To Be' process.

Unlike the 'As Is' process, which is created primarily to enhance the analyst's understanding of what is currently going on, the 'To Be' process is going to end up being something that is owned by the users. This is their process; it represents what the users want to do in the future and they are very much responsible for making sure it does actually represent what they want to do.

Now, the 'To Be' process is often one of the hardest things to define properly. Quite often, the users do not know what they really want to do in terms of a future process. Or they will have a rough idea, but are unsure of the sequence of events that they want to carry out. Or there will be conflicting ideas, people firmly rooted in the way that they currently operate, an unwillingness to change…in fact there could be many reasons why defining the 'To Be' process can be difficult to achieve. This is why we are going to try to make it as easy as possible; by starting with information that we have already obtained, by keeping the initial work at a reasonably high level and by giving the stakeholders something concrete up front that they can review, discuss, reject or approve.

For this exercise, we are going to create part of a 'To Be' diagram describing a future process based on the mathematical modelling example. We will need to use the same process modelling techniques as described in chapter 4 i.e. we will need to use a UML tool or equivalent and will need to create roles and process steps within a swim lane diagram. There is one big difference though… unlike the 'As Is' diagram, we don't actually need to meet with the users to begin creating the 'To Be' diagram!

Instead, we are going to use both the 'As Is' diagram for the mathematical model example and the use case diagram that was created in the last chapter (fig. 31) to create an initial 'best guess' 'To Be' diagram that can be reviewed later with the users. This technique has several advantages:

1. You are creating a starting point for discussion with the users. Working from a blank sheet or just from the 'As Is' process can sometimes be very difficult and time consuming when discussing the future processes with stakeholders.
2. You are controlling the level of detail by keeping it high (at use case level). If you don't do this, your 'To Be' process could end up with a mix of activities at various levels of detail. Discussions with users may end up going off on tangents and / or into too much detail. You will be going into more detail later, but by keeping things at a high level initially you will find you can create the framework for the 'To Be' process much quicker.
3. As you create the initial 'To Be' diagram you will be able to formulate a list of questions that you need to ask the users to fill in the gaps. Attempting to draw the diagram yourself **without** user input will quickly reveal the gaps in your knowledge and trigger a lot of questions that need to be asked about the process.

Okay, let's get started! The first thing to do is to create a new process diagram and add in the swim lanes that represent the roles. You should be able to use the roles from the use case diagram(s) that were created when identifying the functionality needed. If we were to take the mathematical model example that we worked on in the last chapter, we would have a process diagram with only two swim lanes - the senior scientist and the modeler. However, our example in the last chapter was unfinished and in a real-life situation we would have created a use case diagram for each of the roles defined in the 'As Is' process diagram for this example e.g.:

Modeler

Senior Scientist

Field Trial Coordinator

Field Trial Assistant

Next, we need to take another look at the 'As Is' process diagram alongside all of the use case diagrams that were defined. We are effectively examining the current process and comparing each step against the equivalent functionality identified in the use case diagrams. Normally you would start at the beginning of the 'As Is' process and work your way to the end, but for the purpose of this example we are going to imagine that the 'To Be' process we are interested in begins with the field trial assistant sending results to the modeler. This is going to be our starting point. Let's take another look at this part of the 'As Is' process:

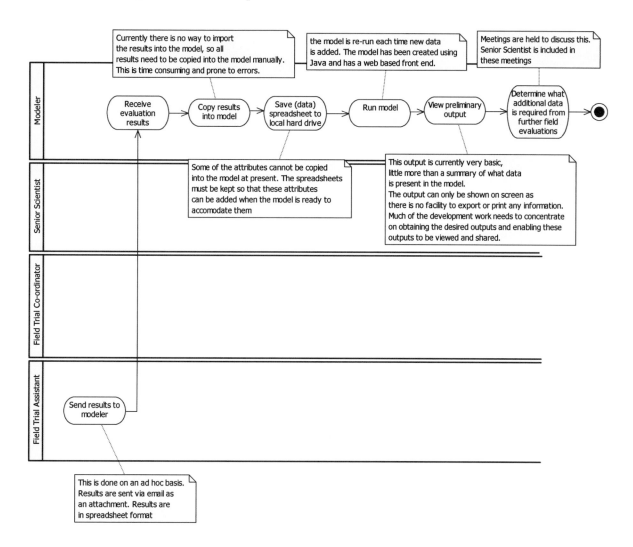

We do not have a use case diagram available for the field trial assistant, but we can make a fairly safe assumption that the results will still need to be send to the modeler in the future. We do have a use case diagram for the modeler (fig. 31), so we will concentrate on describing the 'To Be' process for the modeler in this example.

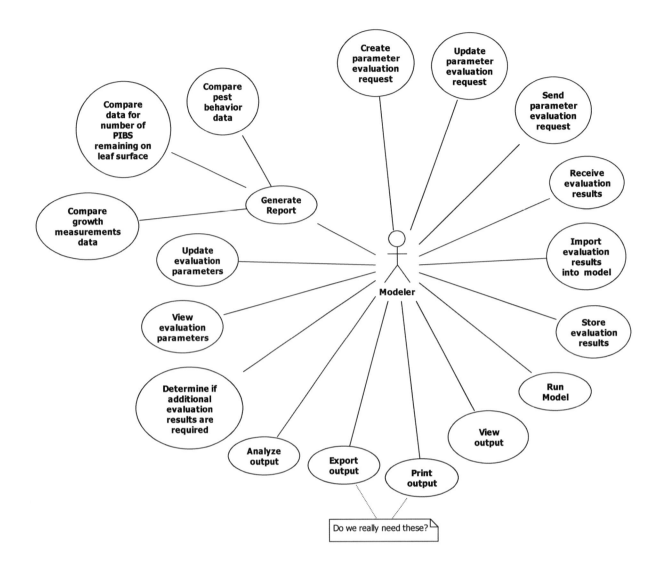

Assuming that results have been sent to the modeler, the first thing the modeler does in the 'As Is' process is receive the evaluation results. Looking again at the use case diagram, we can see that 'receive evaluation results' is a piece of functionality that the modeler needs to do. So it is highly likely that the 'To Be' process for this step is identical to the 'As Is' process.

The next step in the 'As Is' process describes the modeler copying results manually into the model. However, the use case diagram does not mimic this piece of functionality. Instead, we have a use case that states 'import evaluation results into model'. So the 'To Be' process at this step is likely to change. Because the use case diagram was drawn to show the order of the functionalities in a clockwise direction, this should make it easier to compare process steps in the 'As Is' diagram with their equivalent (or new) functionalities in the use case diagram. As you make the comparison between the two diagrams, you should be creating your 'To Be' diagram at the same time. If we were to continue with the comparison between the 'As Is' process diagram and the use case diagram for the next few process steps, we would probably end up with a diagram such as the one shown in fig. 33:

Fig. 33 – Initial 'To Be' process for the mathematical model example (part 1):

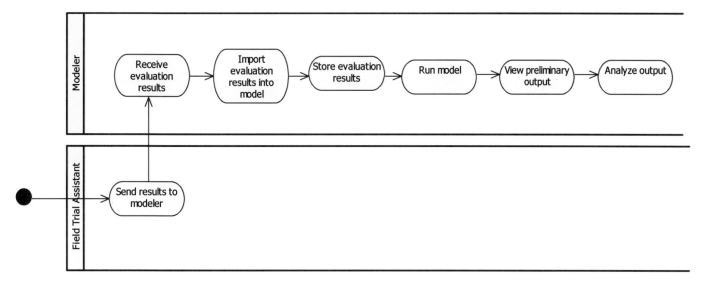

So far so good. To create the 'To Be' process diagram, all we've effectively done is to substitute some of the steps described in the 'As Is' process with steps describing the functionality from the use case diagram. Because the steps and functionality were closely matched, only the original wording of some of the steps in the 'As Is' process has changed. We have added a new activity from the use case diagram – 'analyze output'. We have also removed two roles from the diagram that are not needed for this example - the senior scientist and the field trial coordinator. We have not included any notes. Everything else looks roughly the same as the 'As Is' process.

As we continue, I am going to break the complete diagram down into two parts to make it easier to view on the page. Part 1 will be shown in fig. 33 and part 2 will be shown in fig. 34. If your 'To Be' process diagram is in danger of becoming very large or the process is describing two or three completely different but related concepts; breaking the diagram down into several diagrams is often a good option.

Moving on to the second part of the 'To Be' process, things become a little trickier. This is the part that is mostly new; the outputs from the model are not currently being generated so all the reporting and probably the viewing and updating of parameters which is described in the use cases is not currently being done. So we know 'what' (in terms of functionality) the modeler wants to do in the future. What we don't know is the sequence in which these activities will occur and what it is that will trigger each of these activities. So we are going to have to make an educated guess...

Fig.34 - Initial 'To Be' process for the mathematical model example (part 2):

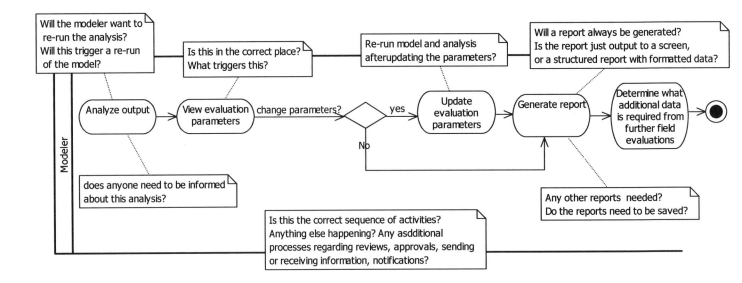

To create this latter part of the diagram we have made the following assumptions:

1. After the initial analysis of the output we think that the modeler will want to view the evaluation parameters, but this is just a logical guess. It might equally well take place before the output is analyzed.
2. We think there may be a decision involved - whether or not to update the parameters. They may or may not be updated depending on what the modeler wants to do at this point.
3. We think generating a report comes towards the end of the process.

Now, none of these assumptions are necessarily correct. This 'To Be' process we've created is just a complete guess, a type of 'mock-up' (a model used to enhance or generate understanding of something). However, it was possible to draw it fairly quickly because it was based on the functionalities in the use case diagram. And by creating this as a 'best guess', it has stimulated a number of questions that need to be put to the users, which we have documented in the form of notes on the diagram. You could if you wish compile a list of questions separate to the diagram… it's up to you. Make sure that when you are creating this draft diagram you are also thinking (for each process step) about any possible interactions that might take place between roles. Example interactions might include sending or receiving something or reviewing or approving something; basically anything involving some form of communication between two or more roles. You will not know if there is any communication involved until you speak to the users, but it is worth making a note to ask them about this.

Another important point - make sure that you keep this diagram simple! It's meant to be used as a starting point for discussion with the users… you do not want anything too elaborate or confusing. The chances are high that the diagram you've drawn is not going to be correct, it will need amending. You might even need to throw it away and start from scratch if it's completely **wrong, so** don't spend too much time trying to make it pretty or accurate; there's no point. Also, make sure you tell your stakeholders up front that this diagram is just a model, a type of mock-up, because that's exactly what it is… it's a model that needs to be worked on to create a proper 'To Be' process.

Obviously, the next step is to talk to the users themselves, using the draft process diagram to stimulate discussion while building on it to create the actual 'To Be' process diagram with the users' participation. This is a very important step, as the information that the users give you during the creation of the 'To Be' process is going to dictate to a large extent what the solution will need to address. Make sure that you keep the diagram high level i.e. roughly at the same level as the use cases. Make sure that you update the use case diagrams with any new functionality that becomes evident from describing the 'To Be' process. Make sure that you also cover the problem statements identified earlier in the approach when discussing the process with the users. Does the 'To Be' process address the issues identified in the problem statements?

There may be circumstances when you will need more than one high level 'To Be' process diagram, for example if you have users in different countries who need to follow different processes in order to achieve the same objective. A case in point may be if the users need to follow different processes to achieve localized regulatory guidelines for a particular country. The objective of creating a 'To Be' process diagram isn't always necessarily about trying to harmonize processes to come up with a single way of working. The key objective here is to show what the users desire to do in terms of process for the future and to show any required disparity if necessary.

Make sure that you capture any requirements, business rules (we'll come on to both of these later) or thoughts about solution while you work with the users to define the agreed 'To Be' process (or processes), but keep these things separate from the process, either as notes recorded against a process step or as notes recorded in a separate document. If any new functionality becomes apparent during these discussions, add it to the functionality (use case) diagram. The same with any new concepts – add them to the business concept diagram. From here on in, all three of these diagrams need to be kept up to date with regards to process, functionality and concepts.

Finally for many types of project including a process improvement project, you will obviously need to go into more detail regarding the 'To Be' process. You still need the high level overview of the 'To Be' process, but you will need to supplement this view with additional detail. We will be coming on to this in chapter 13 – defining the detail for the 'To Be' process. For now though, you should have a fairly high level diagram that describes what the users want to do in the future. The diagram should be agreed with the users and will be owned by those users. The level of detail in this diagram should be roughly at the same level of detail as that used for the use case diagrams.

Chapter 10 – Define the Scope

If you have a high level 'To Be' process that has been agreed with the users, you should be in a good position now to start defining the scope i.e. the extent of the work that is relevant. There are a number of factors to consider when defining the scope, not least of which is who actually defines the scope? You as the analyst are not responsible for defining scope – your job here is basically to help discuss and document what the users, the project sponsor and the development team decide the scope to be. In fact, there are circumstances where all you need to do is just document what has already been decided by someone else e.g. the project sponsor as being 'in scope'. However, different people may have different ideas about what should or should not be in scope, as well as different criteria for defining the scope.

It is a good idea to include a section on scope in your requirements specification document. Even if the scope is documented elsewhere e.g. in a project definition document, make sure that you've also included that scope in your requirements document so that it can be easily referred to by all parties involved, especially the users (who may not necessarily have access to the project documentation). Having the scope clearly defined helps manage user expectations as well as provide a reference point for the work to be carried out. It also give you a very clear idea about what you (and the development team) need to be working on…it provides a focus.

On some projects the scope is defined quite early on, sometimes before either you or the users have a clear idea on what functionality is actually required. The main reason for doing this is to try to get some sort of idea of how much the work is likely to cost, but this initial scoping is not really much more than an educated guess. By talking about scope after you have defined what functionality is required and what the high level 'To Be' process is going to look like, you are in a much better position to start documenting what should be in scope and also, what should be out of scope. Stating what is out of scope is just as important as stating what is going to be in scope.

So, ideally we need to state two things… what is in scope and what is out of scope. We need to discuss scope with both the users and the development team including the project or product manager and possibly a system architect assigned to the work. Let's get started with defining scope by working through an example:

Joe Bloggs has a problem – he needs a new phone. How do we work out what is in scope and what isn't for the Joe Bloggs problem? Basically, we need to look at three things from the stakeholders' viewpoint: the problem, the process and the functionality. We also need to look at three things from the implementation viewpoint: the cost, the complexity and the time to implement. This is why scope has to be agreed by both users and development team – both angles need to be considered to successfully define the scope.

From the users' viewpoint, the scope should address at least some of the critical problems documented in the problem statements. If we look at the problem statements for the Joe Bloggs example back in chapter 5, figure 13, we see the root cause of Joe Bloggs problems as being:

He's unemployed, he's lost his phone, he has no access to a camera, his old phone used a slow processor and it did not provide the extra functionality that is available in a more modern phone.

Some of this will be in scope and some will not. Replacement of the phone will definitely be in scope. Finding Joe Bloggs a job is definitely out of scope. Do we need to state everything that is out of scope? No… this would quickly become ridiculous. You only need to record things that are out of scope when there is a debate or question as to whether or not specific things are in or out of scope – if they are deemed out of scope in discussion then you can record them as being out of scope. If what is going to be in scope is very clear cut then you can make an assumption that everything else not recorded as being in scope is going to be out of scope.

Let's move on to process. Here we only have one key question to ask the stakeholders… 'Is improving the process going to be in scope of the work?' In Joe Bloggs case, his 'As Is' process will change because he doesn't currently own a phone. The process will improve as a consequence of Joe obtaining a new phone, but we are not doing anything to actively improve the process itself… this is not a process improvement project.

Functionality – what functionality should be in scope and what shouldn't? In Joe Bloggs case we would have needed to create a use case diagram to do this properly. However, we can safely assume that in terms of functionality Joe Bloggs wants a phone that can take photographs, play games, send text messages and make phone calls. We don't need to list every piece of functionality that is going to be in scope. Keep it high level unless you specifically want to make clear that a particular piece of functionality has to be in scope.

In terms of the implementation, cost will be a critical factor for most projects but this may or may not affect the scope initially. If there is a set budget and cost is a known limiting factor, it may be a wise move to mention cost up front to manage expectations. The other factor that will affect scope and help manage expectations is time. If you only have a set time to complete the work, you will need to specify what is in scope and what is currently out of scope due to time constraints. Finally, the complexity of the piece of work will also affect the scope. If the development team are shown the list of functionalities that are being considered as within scope, some of these functionalities may be very complex to deliver. This will increase the cost and the amount of time needed, which will raise the question – 'should all of these functionalities be in scope?' To answer this question you may need to help the users prioritize the functionalities in order of importance.

These are basically the key things to consider when defining the scope in your requirements specification document. Keep it simple and high level – you may need to reference and perhaps update the scope later as you move into the future phase – documenting the requirements. However, beware of scope creep! As you get into the detail, things that were not initially considered to be in scope may end up being regarded as necessary to include.

Here is an example of what you might record in the scope section of your requirements specification document:

Fig. 35 – A possible scope for the phone problem example

Scope:

In Scope:

- Selection and provision of a mobile phone that can make calls, take photos, send text messages
- Ability to play 'kill the zombies' game on phone
- Pay as you go phone

Out of scope:

- Contract phone
- Any phone costing more than $200

If we take a look at the more complicated problem of the mathematical model, we might document the scope as being something like this:

Scope:

In Scope:

- Any further development work needed on the mathematical model including work on storage of results data from field evaluations and viewing and analysis of modeling output.
- Provision of an automated data import tool for the model
- Provision of data comparison reports
- Improving the process for the modeler to obtain data from the field evaluations

Out of scope:

- The process for requesting field evaluations

In summary, you are writing the scope in the requirements specification document to make it very clear to all interested parties including yourself, the users and the development team, what work needs to be considered as being 'in scope' and what specific pieces of work need to be classified as being 'out of scope'.

Chapter 11 – Define the Business Requirements

We are now at the point where sufficient information should be available to begin work on defining the future state:

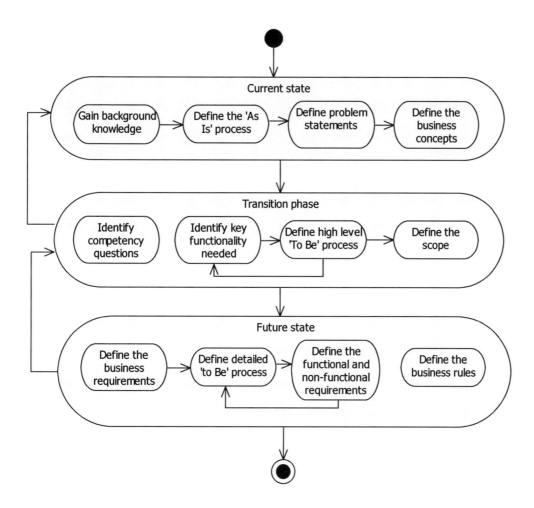

Before we enter this final phase of the approach though, let's just have a quick recap of what we've done so far... because if all has gone successfully to plan you should have come a long way in a relatively short period of time.

You should have a partially filled in requirements specification document that contains some diagrams and perhaps five sections of text. The old saying 'a picture is worth a thousand words' could not be more appropriate, as that is exactly what we have here... several pictures (diagrams) describing various aspects of the problem, including some (high level) ideas about what is required in terms of a solution. We have used several diagrams so far and we will be using several more as we move further into the 'future phase' of this approach. Basically it is much easier to communicate with stakeholders in terms of pictures (diagrams), as opposed to text.

We started with the background, written in just enough detail to give a good understanding of the issues and what the work is meant to be about, putting things into some sort of context. The 'As Is' process diagram was created to provide a good understanding of what is currently going on and to flesh out the problems. The problem statements provided a brief summary of those problems - this is what we are trying to address. We then used the 'As Is' process diagram to create a concept diagram describing the high level concepts and the relationships between these concepts, which also provided us with a common language of defined terms - the glossary. We may well have created a set of competency questions with the stakeholders which provide additional detail on the concepts (and attributes), as well as giving us a pretty clear idea about what sort of querying and reporting is needed.

The 'As Is' process diagram also provided us with a good starting point for another diagram - a high level 'use case' diagram describing the functionalities that would be needed in the future. The 'use case' diagram is used to create an initial 'To Be' process diagram, which is then fleshed out properly with the users. At this point, there should be enough information available to help understand and define the scope...

What we've done so far is to make the process of communication with the stakeholders as straightforward and unambiguous as possible. Assuming each and every step of the approach so far has been carried out (and which steps you actually need to do are dependent on the type of project), you should have five sections of text:

- The background (possibly including a vision statement and high level objectives)
- Some problem statements
- A set of competency questions
- A glossary
- The scope

And you should have between four and six different types of diagram:

- A 'big picture' diagram (possibly)
- One or more 'As Is' process diagrams
- A concept diagram (maybe several depending on the extent of the work)
- A semantic model (possibly)
- One or more use case diagrams
- At least one 'To Be' process diagram

Which takes us finally to talking about requirements. Although requirements have not been specifically mentioned up until this point, it is highly likely that the stakeholders will have already given you some requirements during the 'To Be' definition work and you will already have documented some notes describing these requirements. It is also highly likely that the requirements given to you so far have been a mix of ideas, suggestions and actual requirements, at varying levels of detail. If you have taken notes and identified some potential requirements, now is the time to begin sorting this out.

First though, seeing as this chapter is all about 'business requirements', what exactly do we mean by the term 'business requirement'? Or the term 'requirement' for that matter? The definition of a requirement as we stated in chapter one is pretty straightforward - a requirement is basically a *need* to do something with or to a 'thing'. In the world of business analysis, you may have come across several different types of requirement. Depending on who you speak to, requirements can be functional, non-functional, system requirements, data requirements, technical requirements, user requirements, business requirements, resource requirements, reporting requirements etc. etc. It is easy to become bogged down categorizing various types of requirements, linking one requirement type to another, trying to decide if a requirement is a 'user requirement' or a 'business requirement' or a 'functional requirement'...

I suggest that you just keep it simple. You really don't need to spend a lot of time sorting your requirements into different categories and then linking them all together; it's just going to create confusion. Who is the categorization of requirements actually for? The people who will be looking at these requirements are primarily either the users, vendors (if purchasing a solution), or the development team (including testers). They will be interested in what the requirement states rather than how you have categorized the requirement. Saying that though, you do need to distinguish between three distinct types of requirement:

- Something that is a high level need or objective (business requirement)
- Something that describes the need at a functional or system level i.e. it describes how the thing operates (functional requirement).
- Something that describes the quality or aesthetic needs with regards the solution (non-functional requirement).

We will come on to functional and non-functional requirements later. For now, we are concentrating on business requirements. What I term as a 'business requirement' is basically a high level requirement coming from the business. Many sources describe business requirements as 'the critical activities of an enterprise that must be performed to meet the organizational objectives while remaining solution independent'. I think this is a very apt description of what a business requirement is. The key phrase used in this definition is very important... 'the critical activities of an enterprise'. Now where have we come across something like this before?

The critical activities are effectively the process steps described in the 'To Be' process diagram. These critical activities were derived from functionalities. There is a close correlation between the process steps in the 'To Be' diagram and the required functionality in the use case diagram(s). In other words, each functionality in the use case diagram(s) represents a 'critical activity that must be performed to meet the organizational objectives' or in other words, each functionality is in effect, a business requirement. So by already creating the use case diagram(s) and describing the functionalities needed by the business, we have also identified the business requirements by default!

This is why we need to ensure that the functionalities described in the use case diagrams are kept up to date when defining the 'To Be' process... an up to date set of use cases will help us to define the business requirements.

So what we need to do now is reformat or rewrite the simple functionalities from the use case diagram(s) into properly formatted business requirements. This is a duplication of sorts because the information is already there in the diagram, but this step is necessary for two reasons:

1. Vendors, developers and testers are generally expecting some sort of text to work from – they are used to seeing requirements in text form.
2. The written requirements provide testers with text statements that they can use to create test cases. It saves them time.

I would suggest writing all your requirements in a consistent manner. A requirement has to be clear and understandable and it has to be testable i.e. does the solution address the requirement – yes or no? It should be written in such a way that there is absolutely no ambiguity and this applies to business requirements as well as functional and non-functional requirements.

You could if you wish, write the business requirements out as a set of 'user stories'. We will talk more about user stories later in this chapter, but basically a user story is a requirement that includes three elements: The 'role', the 'doing' part and the 'benefit'. You already have the roles from the use case diagram, so as long as you can include the benefit part of the user story as well, it would be fairly easy to create a set of user stories from the functionalities. We will take a look at doing this in a moment and explain properly what we mean by a 'user story'. The other way of writing out textual business requirements would be to use a fairly standard requirements format such as 'Need the ability to...' for each business requirement. It is worth stating in the requirement *who* needs the ability i.e. the role involved, so in actual fact there is not much difference between writing the business requirements as straightforward requirements statements or as user stories. The main difference is that if you choose to write these requirements as user stories you will need to bear in mind that the requirements derived from this approach are heavily oriented towards functionality. Your user stories will therefore be very functionality biased. Because part of the objective of user stories is to show the value the story provides to the stakeholder, it is very important that you also include the benefits part i.e. the 'value'.

There are a couple more things that are useful to include when documenting business requirements:

- An identifier, so that each requirement can be easily referenced
- A priority, so that each requirement can be prioritized against the other requirements

You could also include information about which user provided you with the requirement. This is more useful at the functional requirement level, but if you have lots of users and you need to keep track of who provided you with the requirement, add it in.

It is a good idea to create a table within the requirements specification document such as the one shown in fig. 36:

Fig. 36 – Example table for displaying business requirements:

Identifier	Requirement	Priority

Let's take another look at the use case diagram in fig. 31 and use that to create a set of conventional business requirement statements:

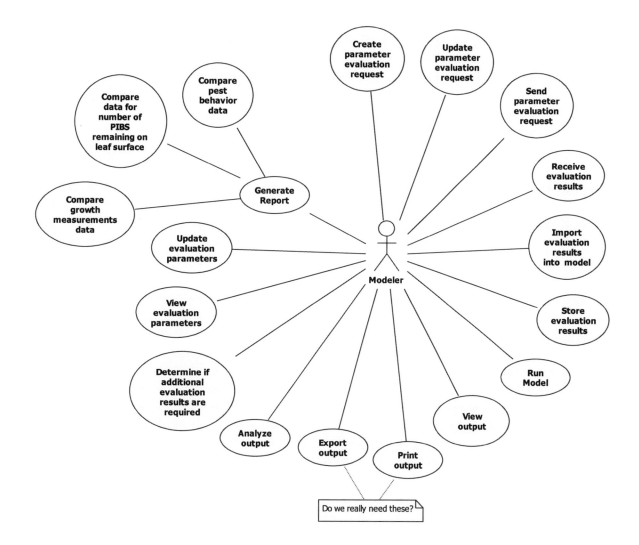

Don't forget, the requirements derived from the use case diagram are based on the functionality that a solution would need to provide. The stakeholders may also provide you with additional business requirements in the form of 'objectives' for what they want to achieve and it is well worth adding these 'objectives' into the requirements specification document as well. You can either list them separately under a section called 'objectives' or add them to the list of business requirements - again it's up to you.

Fig. 37 – Some example business requirements from the mathematical model example:

Identifier	Requirement	Priority
001	Modeler needs the ability to create and send a request for a parameter evaluation to be conducted (in the field)	Medium
002	Modeler needs the ability to receive evaluation results	High
003	Modeler needs the ability to import evaluation results into the model	High
004	Modeler needs the ability to store evaluation results	High
005	Modeler needs the ability to run the model	High
006	Modeler needs the ability to view the output from the model	High
007	Modeler needs the ability to export the output from the model into another tool	Medium
008	Modeler needs the ability to print the output from the model	Low
009	Modeler needs the ability to analyze the output from the model	High
010	Modeler needs the ability to determine if additional evaluation results are required	Medium
011	Modeler needs the ability to view and update evaluation parameters	High
012	Modeler needs the ability to generate reports	High
013	Modeler needs the ability to compare pest behavior data	High
014	Modeler needs the ability to compare data for number of PIBS remaining on leaf surface	High
015	Modeler needs the ability to compare growth measurements data	High

Looking at the above list of requirements, what we've effectively done is to take the simply worded use cases and rephrase them into business requirements, using the phrase 'needs the ability to' as a prefix to the use case. Some additional text has been added to the requirements to make them read better e.g. requirement 1 contains a little more clarification on the parameter evaluation request. When viewing, exporting and printing output, we have clarified which output we are dealing with by adding the text 'from the model'. This provides some context, makes more sense grammatically and leads to better understanding of the requirement.

Requirement 11 is actually a combination of two use cases – view and update evaluation parameters. When talking about the same concept in multiple use cases it can sometimes be useful to combine them into one business requirement…. It makes the list a little shorter and the requirements a little easier to read. Don't forget who the intended audience is for these business requirements and what they are going to be used for… they are not going to be sufficiently detailed enough to build a software system, but they should be detailed and clear enough to provide, for example, information to a vendor describing what is required when purchasing a solution.

Using User Stories to describe business Requirements

I will discuss the pros and cons of user stories versus requirement statements in the next chapter, but for now I'm just going to explain in very simple terms what a user story is and what the above set of business requirements would look like if they were written out as user stories instead of requirement statements. A user story is fundamentally a requirement, in that it describes what someone needs to do. However, it is a little more than just a simple requirement as it includes three elements: The 'role', the 'doing' part (or need) and the 'benefit'. It is actually an extended requirement, written in simple terminology, often by a user, in the format: 'as a (role) I would like to (do something) in order to (stated benefit)'. Again, there are several books available that describe user stories and their use with agile development, so I'm not going to go into much descriptive detail here. Suffice to say, a user story is meant to describe a piece of required functionality using the 'everyday' language of the user. User stories are also used to time-box the development work on agile projects.

If we were to write these business requirements as a set of user stories, they would probably look something like this:

Fig. 38 – Some example business requirements for the mathematical model example:

Identifier	Requirement	Priority
001	As a Modeler, I want to request that a parameter evaluation be conducted in order to use the data for my model	Medium
002	As a Modeler, I want to receive evaluation results so that I can run simulations in the model using these results	High
003	As a Modeler, I want to import evaluation results into the model so that I can run simulations in the model using these results	High
004	As a Modeler, I want to store the evaluation results so that I can re-use them	High
005	As a Modeler, I want to run the model to look at different simulations and scenarios	High
006	As a Modeler, I want to view the output created from the model so that I can compare different simulations and scenarios	High
007	As a Modeler, I want to export the output of the	Medium

	model into another tool in order to compare different simulations and scenarios	
008	As a Modeler, I want to print the output of the model so that I have a hard copy of the output available	Low
009	As a Modeler, I want to analyze the output from the model so that I can compare different simulations and scenarios	High
010	As a Modeler, I need to determine if additional evaluation results are required so that I can request additional work from the field trial assistant	Medium
011	As a Modeler, I need to be able to view and update evaluation parameters in the model so that I can compare different simulations and scenarios	High
012	As a Modeler, I want to generate reports so that I can view the output produced by the model	High
013	As a Modeler, I want to compare pest behavior data in order to provide valuable information on prediction of the effect of baculovirus in the field	High
014	As a Modeler, I want to compare data for number of PIBS remaining on a leaf surface in order to provide valuable information on prediction of the effect of baculovirus in the field	High
015	As a Modeler, I want to compare growth measurements data in order to provide valuable information on prediction of the effect of baculovirus in the field	High

Each user story in the table above has been derived from the use cases in much the same way as the business requirement statements were derived. All that we've done here is to take the basic use case, state which role is carrying out the work and state a reason why the work needs to be carried out - very simple and straightforward. We end up with a high level set of user stories that can be mapped via the use cases back to the process. The users may also provide you with additional user stories (e.g. as a result of discussions during an agile development session) in which case it would be worth checking to make sure that any additional user stories can also be mapped back to use cases. You may need to create more use cases if additional user stories have been identified that indicate functionality that has not already been captured in the use case diagram.

Prioritization of Requirements

In terms of assigning a priority to each requirement, there are several ways to do this. Some analysts use a method called 'MoSCoW' to prioritize requirements. MoSCoW is an acronym for four prioritization categories: 'Must have', 'Should have', 'Could have', and 'Won't have'. I have often had problems working with users in trying to allocate priorities to requirements in this way. The users are well aware that anything deemed as 'Won't have' will not be included in the solution, so they don't voluntarily assign a 'won't have' to a requirement. The difference between a 'must have' and a 'should have' and a 'should have' and a 'could have' is also blurred and very much open to discussion. I don't like to spend time trying to prioritize requirements in this way. If you have several users in the room trying to agree if a requirement is a 'should have' or a 'could have', you are wasting time and running the risk of not even coming to a consensus decision.

I use a 'high', medium, 'low' method of prioritizing requirements. Everyone understands what this means… it's simple and straightforward. High priority requirements are the most important and low priority requirements are the least important. If a stakeholder has taken the trouble to voice a requirement, they want to know that there is at least a chance of that requirement making it into the solution, even if the priority on the requirement is low. Low priority requirements do tend to get dropped if time or money runs out, so these tend to be looked on as 'nice to have' requirements. With a group of users, it is very easy to run quickly through the list of requirements and ask 'is this high, medium or low priority'? About 75% of the time, everyone quickly agrees that the priority is high. If there is uncertainly and a discussion begins, you instantly know that the requirement is probably medium or low priority. You can stop the discussion quickly and ask to assign a medium priority to the requirement. Only in about 5% of cases does the requirement voluntarily get a 'low' priority, unless the users are particularly harsh (or realistic) about their own requirements.

Prioritization of requirements in terms of solution development is a different matter. When you show these requirements to a development team they will probably have an opinion about how the work needs to be prioritized based on time and cost whereas the users should be prioritizing their requirements based on how much they need the functionality. This is important… users prioritize the requirements and the development team state how much it will cost and how long it will take to obtain a solution. Work can then be planned based on all three factors; need, time and cost.

Conclusion

One final point. Now that you have a set of clearly stated business requirements with priorities assigned, you are probably in a good position in terms of understanding to go through the requirements specification document with the development team and use the information in the document to help propose a solution. A basic set of high level business requirements is often enough to help make a vendor selection. In some rare cases, for example when purchasing an 'off the shelf' tool that needs no customization or configuration, you may not have to do much more analysis work on the problem.

You have reached a point where, for problems such as selecting a vendor, investigating a new idea or helping with a departmental 'transformation' project, you may actually have sufficient information for the development team to begin work. For most other types of problem, for example where a new software system needs to be built or an existing system needs to be enhanced, you are going to need to provide a lot more detail.

This is where things might start becoming a little complicated. We have already stated that the business requirements can be documented in two ways: as simple requirement statements or as user stories. As we progress to fleshing out the detail in terms of functional and non-functional requirements, you can also document your requirements as textual use cases. So now there are three ways to document functional requirements. Which documentation method should you use? Should you be documenting all your requirements as one line statements, as textual use cases, or as user stories? Does it even matter? Let's move on to chapter 12 to find out…

Chapter 12 – Documenting Requirements: User Stories *vs.* Use Cases *vs.* Requirement Statements

In chapter 11 we stated that a requirement is a need to do something with or to a thing i.e. a requirement describes something that is needed or wanted. It is very difficult to begin developing a solution if the development team does not know what is needed or wanted, hence rule number 3… requirements before solution. So requirements are needed, and traditionally it has been the job of a requirements engineer or business analyst to elicit and document a set of requirements in order to help propose a solution. But how should these requirements be documented? Do you need to create a set of user stories, or a set of detailed textual use cases, or should you create a long list of functional (and non-functional) requirement statements? It's probably worth at this point, taking a quick look at how things have developed over the last few years in terms of documenting requirements, and this also means taking a very brief look at the waterfall and agile development methodologies as well.

Originally, the requirements engineer or analyst concentrated on creating a list of requirements, usually simple statements formatted similarly to how we formatted the business requirements in chapter 11. Sometimes they would create process (swim-lane) diagrams to complement the requirements, but these diagrams were optional and not intended to be used for anything other than an additional accompaniment to the requirements. Entity relationship diagrams did exist, but were not often used by requirements engineers (the term business analyst did not even exist in those days – we're talking pre-1980's!). The emphasis was on the requirements.

For a long time, requirements were gathered up front, documented and signed off by the users, following a review and approval process. After the requirements had been signed off, no further changes could be made to them unless the change itself went through a 'change management process', which involved reviewing, costing and approving the change. This whole approach is known as 'waterfall methodology' and it has one major advantage and one major disadvantage. The advantage is that you end up with a clearly defined set of requirements that enable the development team to have a good idea about what is required and how long it should take to deliver, along with a fairly good estimate of how much the solution is likely to cost. The disadvantage is that it can all go horribly wrong.

Basically, if you are concentrating solely on gathering a comprehensive set of requirements up front in sufficiently documented detail to develop a solution, it can take a pretty long time. We could be talking months, even in excess of a year. Then, once development work begins and the requirements have become fixed, even more time passes. During that time things can change, requirements can be superseded, they can become redundant or even worse, important requirements might have been missed completely. The analyst would end up with a huge document containing pages and pages of requirements and the users would have to wade through the whole lot to review them. Often, the users would give up, sign their name to the document and hope for the best. Only once the solution was made available to the users could they judge how successfully or poorly the solution would meet their needs. A lot of projects have failed using the waterfall approach, and this failure has often been blamed on deficient or bad requirements.

An entire industry sprang up to try to address this problem. A host of requirement management tools suddenly became available and all sorts of elaborate techniques became *de rigueur*. Requirements were decomposed into various sub-types and had to be linked together in elaborate matrices. However, organizing, categorizing and linking requirements together in expensive requirements management tools didn't really address the problem, although they did create a lot more work for the requirements engineer/analyst.

At the same time these tools were springing up, object oriented development became very popular and UML (unified modeling language) suddenly became the 'next big thing'. UML was a major step forward. This modeling language was designed for both analysts and developers and enabled the two to work very closely together. It was clean, simple and the users could easily understand the diagrams. UML is an excellent means of describing concepts, processes and how a system is intended to function. However, as UML developed from its early beginnings, it became more complex. UML diagrams can be used to generate code, so the more information that is available in the diagrams, the easier it is to generate useful code. UML notation began to expand in order to serve the developer, but the analyst who uses the diagrams solely for analysis work doesn't really need the extra complexity. As an analyst, UML version 2.0 is probably all you need. Subsequent versions of UML are also useable for the analyst, but probably more suited for a developer.

With UML came the idea of use cases. A 'use case' is a series of sequential process (or 'activity') steps carried out by a role (known in UML terminology as an 'actor') to achieve a particular goal. The idea of use cases, invented by Ivar Jacobson in 1992, is pure brilliance. Suddenly, there was a real and valid link between requirements and process. Each step within a use case represents something that the role needs to do… in reality a requirement. By defining a use case you are in effect defining both process and requirements at the same time and tying the two together. This was another major step forward, but unfortunately there was a problem… things were becoming overly complex again.

There are many books out there describing how to write a (textual) use case. Depending on the author, textual use cases can range in complexity from the relatively simple to the extremely complex. Use case text can contain all sorts of additional artifacts such as pre and post conditions, alternative paths, user steps, system steps, inclusions, extensions, triggers, goals… the list goes on. Along with the additional artifacts came the jargon… use cases can be 'brief', 'casual', 'fully dressed' etc. Writing a single 'fully dressed' textual use case could take an analyst the best part of a day. A use case doesn't just contain text though; it can also be represented by a diagram. The diagram, known as an 'activity diagram' is a summary of the activity steps within the use case and is an extremely valuable artifact of the use case.

So a use case is a great thing, it is useful (but potentially very long winded) and it links requirements and process together. However at the end of the day, a textual use case is just another way of writing a list of requirements. Using use cases within a waterfall development methodology does not address the fundamental problems listed above… you still have a set of requirements that need to be signed off before development work can begin and you still run the risk of the requirements changing during development or ending up with a solution that is no longer appropriate. You may potentially spend even more time documenting use cases than a set of simple requirement statements and you still haven't solved the root cause of the problem…requirements are still blamed for the failure of the project.

So then we have 'agile'. Agile development is not actually new…there were agile style methodologies around in the 1980's and 1990's, but it wasn't until 2001 when the 'Agile manifesto' was published that agile really started taking off. At its heart, agile development is really 'iterative' development. Instead of gathering all the requirements up front and then developing a solution using a waterfall methodology, agile development involves developing a solution in bite sized chunks, in an iterative fashion. If requirements change then the solution can be quickly adapted to accommodate the change. Using an agile methodology, small pieces of work could be rapidly developed… it wasn't called agile for nothing. This was rapid solution development and to make it even faster, things became more streamlined and all unnecessary artifacts were stripped out of the methodology. Large requirements documents stuffed to the brim with lists of functional requirements or heavily documented use cases were 'out' and user stories were 'in'.

In chapter 11 we have already defined a user story as being a requirement that includes three elements: The 'role', the 'doing' part and the 'benefit'. However, just like use cases, there are many ways of writing a user story and they can contain lots of additional artifacts depending on what the writer wants to include. A properly written user story designed for agile development should include test criteria as well as the statement that comprises the 'story'.

The big problem with agile development and user stories is that what starts off as being a fundamentally simple and quick methodology for small projects rapidly becomes unmanageable when it needs to be scaled up for larger projects or programs of work. If detailed requirements are gathered in chunk sized bites on the fly, there may be problems joining up these chunks of work into a cohesive whole, especially with a large piece of work. It is absolutely crucial that sufficient analysis work is done up front on large agile projects, else the user stories won't describe the full picture. What you end up with is several disjointed individual pieces of the full picture.

Ideally, user stories need to be linked directly to process in the same way that use cases and requirement statements can be linked to process; but this is often not done. Unlike use cases, user stories cannot be represented graphically, so with a larger project the amount of user stories increases and the users have the same problem they originally had with a list of requirement statements… lots of text to wade through. Because of the nature of a user story… it is written from the perspective of a user using the sort of language that a stakeholder would use… it can often be prone to ambiguity. A user story is also often regarded as transitory i.e. used to 'time-box' development work on an agile project and once that piece of work has been completed, the user story is discarded. If user stories are used in this way it can be difficult or even impossible to track back to the original requirements if something needs to be checked at a later time during development.

To make things even more confusing, there are several different ways to conduct 'agile' development including Scrum and its many variations, Lean, Kanban, Crystal (and variants), Extreme Programming (XP) etc. What are the guidelines for selecting which agile methodology should be followed? What happens if you select the wrong methodology for the type of project you are working on? The concept of iterative development is a good one, but because of the diversity and variability that has been introduced to agile, it can be just as possible to run into difficulties with agile project delivery as it is using a waterfall methodology.

So there doesn't appear to be any one right answer. There are however, certain elements from each of these methodologies and techniques that do stand out as being particularly useful, when considering an approach. With waterfall, the fundamental structure of the requirement as being a simple statement is actually a very good one. Simple statement requirements, if properly written, are clear, understandable, unambiguous and testable. With UML, the basic diagrams such as the activity diagram (for drawing process), the use case diagram (for functionalities) and the class diagram (for drawing concepts) are very useful. These three diagrams have been incorporated into the approach described in this book. With agile, the principle of iterative development is the key thing here... iterative development overcomes the inherent problems of using a waterfall methodology. I would strongly recommend using an iterative approach to development.

In terms of whether or not to use user stories, use cases or simple requirement statements, let's just quickly summarize some of the pros and cons of these three main methods of documenting requirements:

Simple, one sentence requirement statements:

Pros:

- Easy to read, clear, concise and testable (as long as they are written correctly)
- They can be easily translated into test cases.
- They can be easily derived from diagrams – either use case diagrams (for business level requirements) or activity (process) diagrams (for functional requirements).

Cons:

- These need to be written properly or else they can be easily misinterpreted.
- You may end up with hundreds of requirement statements. Asking the stakeholders to review and approve huge lists of requirements introduces another risk – they may be unable or unwilling to spend time doing this.

Use Cases:

Pros:

- Use cases are heavily linked to process and this linkage provides valuable context for the requirements.
- They can contain a lot of valuable detail, including triggers (pre-conditions) and outcomes (post conditions).
- Use cases can show the exploration of alternative scenarios (alternate paths) which helps identify additional requirements that can easily be missed.
- They can be described using an 'activity' diagram as well as by text.

Cons:

- Writing use cases as text documents can take significant time and effort
- Just like requirement statements, these need to be written properly or else they can be misinterpreted.
- Stakeholders are generally not as familiar with textual use cases as they are with requirement statements. This unfamiliarity can cause issues when stakeholders are asked to review the use cases.
- Use cases are generally not seen as being part of an agile methodology. The development team may not accept use cases if you are working on an 'agile' project.

User Stories:

Pros:

- Designed to allow developers to swiftly produce a solution in an iterative fashion, creating bite sized chunks of functionality based on one or more user stories.
- Supposedly easy for a user to understand (and write)
- Provides additional information on why a requirement is needed i.e. the benefit (as long as this portion is written as part of the user story)
- Provides a useful set of test criteria up front (as long as this portion is written as part of the user story).

Cons:

- Can become just as textually bloated as a use case if certain standards are adhered to when writing the user stories
- Often regarded as 'transitory' i.e. throw-away. This makes it difficult to maintain a set of requirements for checking back on post development, or for re-use.
- You may end up with hundreds of user stories for a large project. It can be difficult to relate these user stories to process and see where the story fits in context of the 'big picture'.

- Just like requirement statements, these need to be written properly or else they can be easily misinterpreted. Due to the casual way a user story is formatted, it is very easy to introduce ambiguity to the requirement.

There are undoubtedly more pros and cons for each of these techniques, but this is enough for me to make some suggestions:

1. I would suggest first of all that you do not use textual use cases. It takes too long to write them, the stakeholders may have problems understanding them and you can easily become bogged down in the detail.

2. Having said that, I think the use cases themselves (represented in a use case diagram) are extremely useful for showing the functionality that is required by a role. This is part of the approach as described in chapter 11. Moreover, I think the activity diagrams that show the process flow within a use case are absolutely imperative if you want to document functional requirements quickly. I will cover this as part of the approach in the next chapter.

3. I do not see a significant advantage in using user stories over requirement statements. A 'fully dressed' user story is just as bloated as a 'fully dressed' use case and user stories (currently) cannot be described within a diagram. Nor is it easy to relate user stories to process without additional traceability work on the part of the analyst.

4. Having said that, I think that by following the approach as described in this book it can be just as easy to relate user stories to process as it is to relate requirement statements to process. If a user story is made equivalent to a business requirement and a test criteria is made equivalent to a functional requirement, then user stories and test criteria can be easily derived from use cases (functionalities) and activity diagrams.

5. I would suggest that if you don't particularly need to create user stories, you should document your requirements using simple requirement statements that can be easily derived from use case and activity diagrams. However, if you do need to create a set of user stories because you are working on a project that uses an agile development methodology or if you have a personal preference for writing user stories and test criteria, there is absolutely no reason why you can't do this when following the approach described in this book.

6. I would also suggest that you avoid having your users review long lists of textual requirement statements or user stories. Instead, they should review the workflow (activity) diagrams that describe each use case and use the textual requirements for reference.

In summary, avoid writing textual use cases. Create user stories if you prefer this method of documentation or you have to document user stories as part of an agile development methodology. Alternatively (and this is just my personal preference), try to stick to clear, simple testable requirement statements and make sure that you review the use case and activity diagrams with the users rather than a huge list of requirements. Which leads us nicely on to the next chapter, where I will show you how this can be easily achieved.

Chapter 13 – Define the Detailed 'To Be' Process (in terms of workflows)

Before we can actually begin documenting the more detailed (functional) requirements as either textual single line statements or as acceptance criteria belonging to user stories, we actually need to conduct some further work on the 'To Be' process. The approach described in this book follows the principle that functional requirements can be derived from the process; more specifically they can be derived from the activity diagrams that show the workflow within each use case (functionality).

A workflow is a series of activities (operations or actions) that are necessary to complete a task. Each piece of functionality that is of interest will have its own workflow i.e. a series of action steps that are carried out in order to achieve the task described by the functionality (use case). The diagram that describes a workflow is known as an 'activity diagram' in UML terminology and we will also be referring to these diagrams as 'activity diagrams' in this book.

Use cases in themselves are a great idea but as already stated in the previous chapter, the textual description of a use case can be very time consuming to properly document and in my experience, some users are not comfortable when reviewing the text. So we are going to use the diagrammatical aspect of the use case... the workflow itself as represented within an activity diagram, to help us document the functional requirements. As well as being used to derive the functional requirements, the activity diagrams are also used to describe the future ('To Be') process in greater detail. The extra detail and clarity provided by these diagrams is absolutely crucial for many projects, including process improvement.

So let's get started! Again, we will use the mathematical model example to illustrate this part of the approach. Here is the use case diagram again from fig. 31:

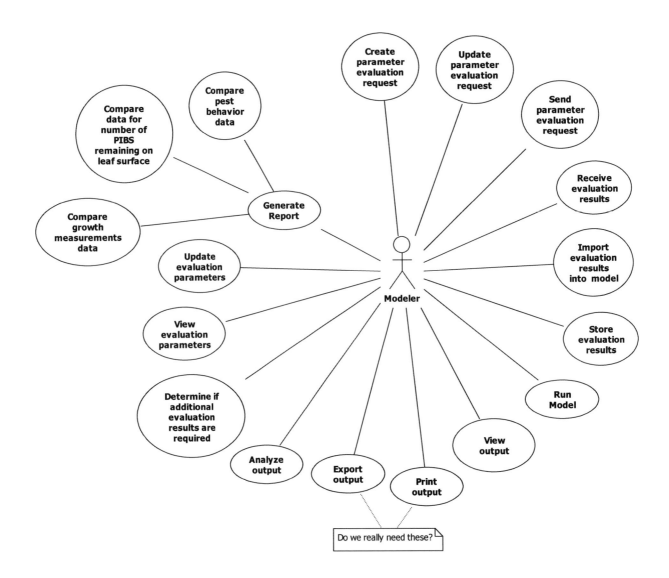

What we are going to do is to create a workflow (activity) diagram for each of these use cases (functionalities). A couple of points to note here:

1. We are only interested in functionality that has been agreed to be in scope. There may be use cases on the diagram that are not in scope, for example creating a parameter evaluation request. If this is the case, it is worth checking on what has already been defined as being in or out of scope. We do not want to waste time drawing up process diagrams for functionality that is out of scope.

2. The use case diagram must correlate with the high level 'To Be' process that has been agreed with the users. These two diagrams must be in synch, i.e. if there is additional functionality mentioned in the 'To Be' process then that functionality must also appear in the use case diagram. Likewise, if there is functionality in the use case diagram that is irrelevant to the 'To Be' process, it should be removed.

3. We can use 'patterns' to create some of these activity diagrams up front. There are certain pieces of functionality that tend to follow a certain pattern when describing what happens in terms of process, especially with regards to software development. If for example we want to create a data object, we can safely assume that you will need to record some attributes against the data object and you will need to save whatever details you have recorded. We will cover this in more detail as we create some example diagrams.

It is always good to have something ready to present to the users that they can review, rather than attempting to start from a blank sheet of paper. As has already been mentioned when creating the 'To Be' process – it focuses their attention and reduces ambiguity - it's either correct or it isn't. If it isn't correct you can correct it. If things need adding you can add them. If the users aren't sure if it's correct or if something needs adding, then it becomes a topic for discussion. So where (and if) possible, you should try to create a draft diagram first, then check it through with the users, just like we did for the high level 'To Be' process.

Now, in a lot of cases it may not be possible to create a diagram first for review with the users. You may have to set up a series of meetings and work through each activity diagram directly with the users, unless you are fairly confident that you can create a useful starting point by using a 'pattern'. It can also be very useful to search for similar work that has been done before on the subject… either within the company you are working for or external to that company i.e. in available literature on the internet. The chances are high that unless what you are working on is a completely new and innovative idea, similar work has been done before. Let's face it, the Bible had it right all those years ago when it was written (Ecclesiastes 1:9) "What has been will be again, what has been done will be done again; there is nothing new under the sun". Try to re-use as much as possible.

Going back to our use case diagram and navigating clockwise around it from the top, the first use case is 'request parameter evaluation' so we'll start with this one as our initial example, assuming that this functionality is indeed within scope. We will begin by creating a new activity diagram and if you are using a UML tool such as StarUML then you can create the diagram from the use case itself, thereby automatically associating the process with the functionality. Unlike the other process diagrams we have created so far, the high level 'As Is' and 'To Be' diagrams, we don't particularly need to use swim-lanes for this one. A swim lane diagram is very useful if you are describing a process that has multiple roles. Because we are delving down into a lower level of detail and concentrating on a specific piece of functionality, the likelihood of the process having multiple roles is reduced. So a simple diagram with activities drawn from top to bottom should suffice e.g.

Fig. 39 – Example activity diagram for the 'request parameter evaluation' use case (first draft):

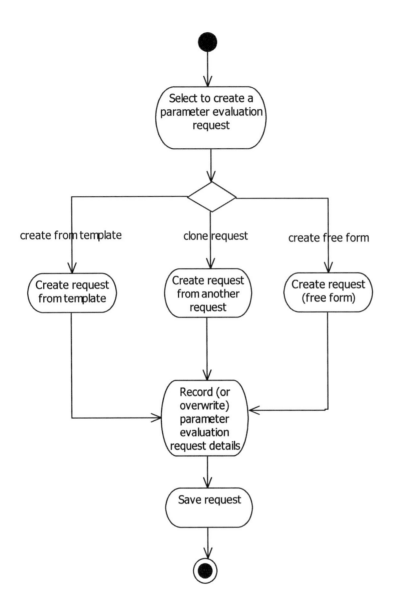

Using patterns

To create this diagram without any stakeholder input, we have used a 'pattern' (in this case a 'create' pattern), which is basically common sense logic. We have an object... in this case a request. The request has to be created. The request consists of some information that will need to be recorded against the request, and that information will need to be saved. Because it's a request, it needs to be sent to someone. So far, so logical. We have two questions... are we going to use some sort of template to create the request and what information do we actually need to record to describe the request?

A common 'create' pattern is to think about the various ways something can be created. Let's take an example: creating a model robot from Lego bricks. Assuming you have the bricks available, you can create it completely from scratch, using your imagination. Or you can take an already built robot and alter the design of the robot so that you are effectively creating a new robot. Or you can follow a pre-designed template that serves as a set of instructions for creating the robot. You then assemble the components (in this case the bricks) necessary to create the robot until the robot is finished. You can then keep the robot, or smash it to pieces if you prefer.

Likewise in the world of software, you can create the object free-form i.e. from scratch. Or you can copy (clone) an existing object and amend it, or you can use some sort of template to record information (e.g. with pre-defined attributes). The assembling of components is basically recording the necessary information about the object. You can then keep (save) the object, or delete it (don't save) as the case may be. Every time an object needs to be created you can use the 'create' pattern; which in its most basic form looks like this:

1. Select to create (the object)
2. Create using a template, a copy of a pre-existing object, or free form?
3. Assemble components (record information)
4. Save (or don't save)

Remember, a pattern is just for use as a starting point – there will always be additional details that need to be considered when you talk to the users. For example, does any of the information recorded need to be validated (either manually or automatically) at time of entry? Are there any calculations that need to be performed? What about keeping an audit trail for changes? Whenever you use a pattern to create an activity diagram, you need to show the diagram to the users and ask them questions to supplement the basic information. The users have to provide you with a complete picture of the process that they want (or need) to follow.

If we were to show this very basic diagram to the users and use it to focus discussion on what the process for creating a parameter evaluation request needs to look like, we might end up with a completely different diagram after the meeting:

Fig. 40 – Example activity diagram for the 'request parameter evaluation' use case (after discussion with the users):

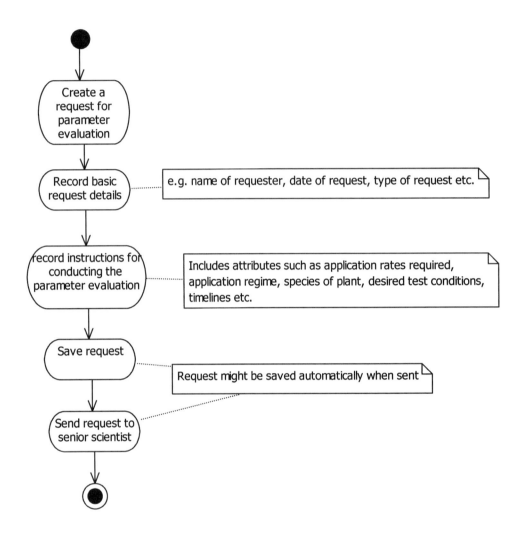

Notice that in the diagram above, we no longer have a decision point where the users choose to create a request from a template, or from a cloned request. In our theoretical meeting, the users did not want to create a request using a template, they wanted to continue creating requests in a 'free form' manner. This could happen… sometimes the users can make decisions that you as an analyst do not think are logical. You have every right to challenge them though!

Which other activity diagrams from the mathematical model example can we easily create using patterns? Let's try the next one… 'Receive evaluation results'. Here we have an object that in order to be received, has to first have been sent. It probably has to have been sent from someone else, unless it's something you are sending to yourself... Either way we're dealing with two roles here – a sender and a receiver, and also two patterns, a send pattern and a receive pattern.

In terms of the receive pattern, when you are about to receive something you probably want to be informed that the object is on its way, so that you are prepared to receive it. You may also want to know when it was dispatched and who sent it, so that you can track it if it goes missing. However, these activities are not crucial to the process of receiving an object. You can ask the users if these activities need to be included within the process, but the pattern itself does not need to include these activities.

What do I mean by this? Basically, I am saying that a pattern needs to be very simple. A pattern should only contain the activity steps that are absolutely crucial for the process to be carried out. Think of a pattern as the basic framework around which you need to ask further questions in order to flesh out the detail. The pattern is intended to give you a starting point for documenting the process, but it should not be used to steer the users in a certain direction. You may be able to think of several steps that might be required for the process, but unless they are crucial to the process then I would suggest that you leave them out of the diagram. You can ask the users if these additional steps are required when reviewing the diagram, but I would recommend that if you do use patterns to create some activity diagrams up front, keep them very simple and straightforward.

So, going back to the receive pattern, you probably only need to consider four steps. It's usually a good idea to begin the pattern with a step describing what it is you are selecting to do. If you are describing an operation that will be performed using software, it is highly likely that the user will need to make some sort of selection, for example by clicking on an icon, in order to begin the operation. So I usually include a 'select' step as the first step in a pattern. The user then needs to carry out the operation i.e. receive the object. What will the user do with the object once it's been received? The user will need to put it somewhere and check to make sure that it's complete and correct. So it is possible to describe a receive process using a pattern; e.g.:

1. Select to receive (the object)
2. Receive object
3. Store object
4. Check object to ensure that it is valid

I have included a list of some common patterns in Appendix 1 at the end of this book, along with a list of things to consider (questions to ask the users) when using a pattern. However, it is up to you as the analyst as to whether or not you use patterns to help with the analysis. I personally find them to be very useful. They provide a starting point and a focus for discussion, they are re-usable and they allow you to remain one step ahead in your analysis work.

The 'what' and the 'how'

Another point to note… when you create an activity diagram from a pattern, you are only describing the 'what'. If we take the receive pattern as an example, 'how' you receive an object is a different matter entirely. In terms of the results that are being received in the 'receive evaluation results' use case, there are various ways these evaluation results can be received. They could be sent electronically as an attachment in an email, they could be sent automatically from a data capture tool, they could even be sent as a paper copy through the post. The patterns will only help establish the 'what'. When you get to this level of detail it is also worth considering the 'how' as well because there may be important requirements describing specifically how something needs to be carried out that could restrict or dictate the solution design. The best way to think about the 'how' is to think about it in terms of 'constraints' (limitations or restrictions). We will come on to this in more detail in the chapter on functional requirements, but for now it is well worth noting down any 'constraints' that appear from discussions with the users. If the users can only receive the results in the form of a paper copy then this is a constraint i.e. a limitation or restriction. If they want in the future to receive the results automatically from another system, this can also be regarded as a constraint. The 'what' is the pure requirement. The 'how' is a constraint imposed on the requirement.

Let's imagine that for the purposes of this example, the modeler want the modelling tool to receive the evaluation results directly from the sender, i.e. the results need to go straight into the modelling tool and will be stored there. The modeler also wants to be notified automatically when the results are received. The results can then be checked manually to make sure that the data is valid. Now, this may or may not be possible to implement, but this is the process the users (in particular the modeler) want to follow, so these are the requirements (which can of course be challenged!). The resulting diagram after discussion with the users may look something like this:

Fig. 41 - Example activity diagram for the 'receive evaluation results' use case:

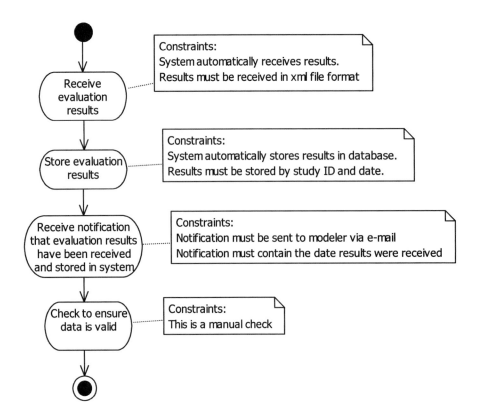

A final example

We will just take a quick look at one more use case example to finish off here. The next use case is 'import evaluation results into model'. This one is also pretty straightforward in that there are only a limited number of possibilities in terms of process when you import (or export) something. We can use a pattern for this one as well e.g.:

Fig. 42 – Example activity diagram for the 'import evaluation results into model' use case (first draft):

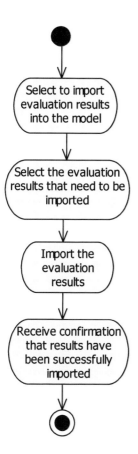

Now, this diagram is a good example of one that may end up generating further discussion with the users. Firstly, how does this process fit alongside the 'Receive Evaluation Results' process? The receive process describes receiving and storing the results. This process describes selecting results to be imported into the modeling tool. Are the two processes complementary or contradictory? Are they actually describing the same process using different terminology for the same thing? Do we still need this process if the results have been automatically received and stored in the tool? Probably not.

Let's assume though, that for the sake of this example the modeler does still want to import results into the tool manually. Maybe the modeler has obtained some results from another source or they are results that have not been sent automatically. If this is the case, you might still end up with both a 'Receive Evaluation Results' activity diagram and a separate 'Import Evaluation Results into Model' diagram. It's quite possible.

The other thing to consider is that in addition to an import process carried out by a modeler, you would probably also have an export process carried out by a Field Trial Assistant. This would fit nicely with the 'Receive Evaluation Results' process i.e. the results are being exported by the field trial assistant (maybe prompted by the manual press of a button for example) and received by the modeling tool automatically. Or alternatively, an export and import process rather than an export and receive process… lots to discuss with the users! On top of these questions you will also need to make sure that you ask about the other considerations documented in appendix 1.

Summary

Getting these activity diagrams right is very important. This is where you are defining not only what the users want to do in the future in terms of process, but also (ultimately) the functional requirements and constraints that will help define the solution. This is requirements elicitation but conducted using diagrams, in a rapid, straightforward and unambiguous manner. This is where you as an analyst need to probe for and coax out the information from the users, but in a structured fashion that relates directly to the process.

For each use case that is within scope in your use case diagram, you will need to create a detailed activity diagram. If the activity diagram starts becoming too large, break it down into two (or more) activity diagrams. Usually if this happens, the functionality described in the use case diagram may be at too high a level, or the workflow you are describing may be highly complex. If the process needs to differ between groups of users, show that in the diagram, or use multiple diagrams to describe the differences for that piece of functionality.

In conclusion, it is possible to create a starting point for discussion with the users (for certain use cases) using patterns. During the ensuing discussions with the users (where you will be confirming, refining or redrawing these diagrams), you will also need to add notes (where relevant) to the processes in order to provide any additional information or detail that comes out of the discussions. You will need to capture any mention of 'how' the stakeholders want to work in the future as 'constraints'. The whole purpose of this exercise is to describe the 'to be' process in sufficient detail in order that functional requirements can be generated from the process steps. And this is what we are going to take a look at in the next chapter – defining the functional requirements.

Chapter 14 – Define the Functional Requirements

In previous chapters we have already mentioned a little about functional requirements, but we have not explored the concept of what a functional requirement really is in any great detail. Now though is the time to begin looking at what a functional requirement actually is and how it should be properly documented. We have said earlier that a requirement is basically a need to do something with or to a 'thing', and a business requirement is a high level requirement coming from the business. A functional requirement can be looked on as being different to a business requirement in that a functional requirement describes the need at a functional or system level i.e. it describes how something is intended to operate (functionally).

Let's take a very simple example to explain the difference between a business requirement and a functional requirement. Remember Joe Bloggs and his lost phone? We haven't mentioned him for a while... but in terms of a business requirement he wants to make a phone call. He wants to send a text message. He wants to play a game. These are business requirements... they can almost be viewed as high level objectives; something that a stakeholder wants to achieve. Business requirements can also be equated to the use cases (functionalities) that are described on a use case diagram.

A functional requirement describes a single operation (or activity) that needs to be carried out in order to help meet a business requirement. It basically describes an interaction, either between the stakeholder and an object (thing) or a system and an object. A functional requirement equates to an activity that is carried out as part of the process for describing what needs to happen to make the business requirement possible. In chapter 13 we discussed how to define the workflows for each of the functionalities (use cases) by creating an activity diagram for each use case. Each step (activity) in these activity diagrams equates to a functional requirement.

One more very important point - a functional requirement must be completely independent of the solution. There should be no mention of solution in the wording of the requirement even if it is blatantly obvious what the solution is going to be. Why is this so necessary? Two main reasons:

1. You are making an assumption by stating the solution up front and this can be a very dangerous thing to do. Requirements should express a fundamental need; they are designed to address a particular problem; they should not be tied to a solution.
2. A good requirement should be re-usable. You can save time and effort by re-using requirements from other projects if that requirement expresses the same fundamental need.

Going back to the phone example, in terms of functionality, what does Joe Bloggs need to do when he makes a phone call? Well, he probably wants to be able to input or dial a number. He may want to select a number that can be dialed at the press of a button. He wants the call to connect to the recipient of the call and he wants some sort of response – either the receiver of the call answers or the caller is informed that the recipient is unavailable. If we drew this as an activity diagram it would look something like this:

Fig. 43 - Example activity diagram for making a phone call:

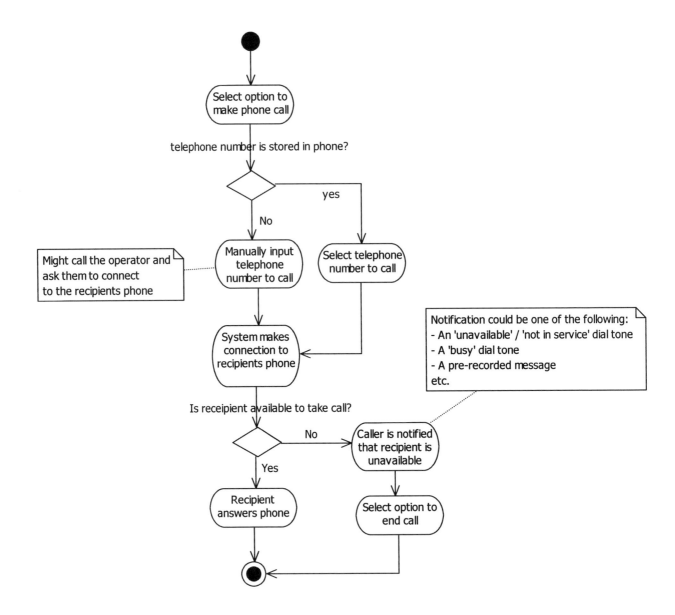

Each of these activities describes an operation that occurs when a stakeholder (in this case Joe Bloggs) interacts with something (in this case a phone). The system itself can also be regarded as a type of stakeholder, so functional requirements may relate to operations performed by the system as well as by a person. We can take the diagram above and create a functional requirement from the text of each activity step in the same way that we took a use case and created a business requirement from the text of the use case:

Fig. 44 – Example table of functional requirements for making a phone call:

Identifier	Requirement	Priority
001	Phone user needs the ability to make a phone call	High
002	Phone user needs the ability to manually input a telephone number to call	High
003	Phone user needs the ability to select a telephone number to call	High
004	System needs the ability to make a connection to recipients phone	High
005	If recipient is unavailable, phone user needs to be notified by the system that recipient is unavailable	High
006	Phone user needs the ability to end the call	High

Now, how you word the functional requirement is up to you, but within limits. You could use the phrase as above – 'needs the ability to' in front of each activity. Or you could use 'must have the ability to…' or 'must be able to…' etc. The requirement has to be written so that there is no chance of misinterpreting it. The requirement must also be unambiguous. If you use words like 'should' e.g. 'phone user *should* have the ability to make a phone call', the requirement becomes less strong and more open to interpretation, so avoid the use of the word 'should' in your requirements. Try to use strong words like 'must', 'will', 'need' in your requirements. Try to keep the requirement to a single sentence. If you need to elaborate on the requirement and write more than a single sentence… don't. I will explain in a minute how to elaborate on a requirement without writing several sentences of text. Keep the requirement short and to the point. You have to potentially be able to ask the following question of each requirement…

'If you were to test to see if a solution can meet this requirement, does the check yield a 'yes / no' answer?' In other words, each requirement you write must be testable… you must be able to specify if the solution does or does not meet the conditions asked for in the requirement.

Now, you will probably find that some of the requirements collected by going through the activity diagrams do not contain sufficient detail for developing a solution. These are effectively placeholders for further work… if you tried to include all the detail at this stage you would be using a 'waterfall' approach and this is something I would recommend you avoid… you are better off documenting a good set of high level functional requirements and revisiting them in an iterative manner during the development phase. You can however, perform some basic elaboration on the requirements by using three very specific techniques. The first of these techniques can be applied to any requirement and will help to dramatically flesh out the requirement. The second technique is needed when you have a requirement that needs to be broken down to a lower level of granularity and the third technique is specific to the inputting or outputting of information / data (i.e. an alternative means of documenting 'data' requirements). We will come on to the latter two techniques in a minute - the first technique I want to discuss with you is about documenting 'constraints' for your requirements.

Constraints

A constraint is a limitation or restriction. When combined with a requirement, it provides a very powerful means of helping flesh out the requirement. When you want to elaborate on a requirement and provide some more detail, don't use additional sentences of text – use constraints.

Constraints can include anything that will affect or influence the solution; for example shape, colour, time, location, quantity etc. Constraints are also very useful when describing the appearance of something i.e. how a user would like something to be displayed. This can be particularly useful when describing things like user interfaces and reports, which I will cover in a later chapter.

Let's take an example from one of the requirements written in fig. 44: 'Phone user needs the ability to manually input a telephone number to call'. We have taken this requirement straight from one of the process steps in the activity diagram. Although it's written as a one sentence functional requirement and it's testable (can the phone user manually input a telephone number – yes or no?) and a developer could probably address it without too many questions being asked, it might help to provide some additional detail i.e. give some additional elaboration using constraints.

Fig. 45 – Example functional requirement with constraints:

002	Phone user needs the ability to manually input a telephone number to call Constraints: • Number can include the digits 0-9 • Number can include the characters * (star), # (hash) • Must be possible to input up to 30 digits and characters when making the call • Etc.	High

A constraint needs to be written in the same way that a requirement is written i.e. it needs to be short, understandable and testable. The purpose of using constraints is to limit the scope of the requirement and to provide valuable information that can be used by the development team. You will probably not be able to identify all of the constraints for each requirement up front and you don't need to. There is no point in trying to list every possible constraint for each requirement... you only need to write constraints when the requirement needs them, usually during the development phase and usually in response to one or more questions from the development team. If you already have additional information from the users regarding particular requirements you can try to pre-empt questions from the development team by writing constraints against those functional requirements that you think will require more detail.

Granularity

This is the second technique – breaking the requirement down to a lower level of granularity. A good example of a requirement that will need to be broken down into a lower level of granularity is the example requirement 005 from fig. 44:

005	If recipient is unavailable, phone user needs to be notified by the system that recipient is unavailable	High

Now, there could be more to this requirement than meets the eye because there are several scenarios where the recipient of a phone call may be unavailable:

1. The recipient may be on the phone to someone else i.e. the phone is engaged
2. The recipient may have set an answering machine to respond with a message after several rings
3. The recipient may not have set an answering machine to respond and the phone may cut out after numerous rings
4. The recipient can't be bothered to answer the call
5. The recipients phone line is disconnected

Etc.

When you come across a requirement like this, you don't want to write an entire essay describing the situation. You could draw up a single, activity diagram to include all the different scenarios but this might look quite complicated. Ideally, you need to break this requirement down, and the chances are high that the breakdown of this requirement needs to be documented at the business level as well i.e. on the use case diagram.

So let's take a step backwards and show what might happen when a phone user makes a call and that call is not answered by the recipient. In the first scenario where the phone is engaged, the phone user (caller) will know that the phone is engaged because the phone is emitting a number of continuous beeps. These beeps are notifying the caller that the phone is engaged. The next scenario describes the use of an answering machine. The answering machine will notify the caller that the recipient of the call is not available. In scenarios three and four, nothing happens to notify the caller that the recipient is not available. The caller has to assume the recipient is not there as the phone was not answered. In the fifth scenario, the phone user may hear the voice of an operator telling the caller that the phone is no longer in use i.e. disconnected. Or the caller may hear a long continuous tone that indicates disconnection. Either way, this is a form of notification. We can describe these different ways of notifying a phone user that a recipient is unavailable in the form of a use case diagram:

Fig. 46 – Example use case diagram showing what happens when a call is not answered by the recipient:

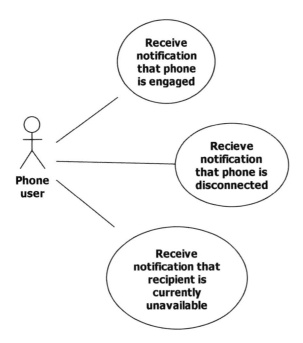

Notice that the third use case does not state 'receive notification from answering machine that recipient is unavailable'. An answering machine is a solution and we cannot assume that this is the solution that will be used for sending a notification of unavailability to the phone user. We already know from scenario four that the recipient of the call might not want to pick up the phone, so the notification of unavailability might take the form of the phone continuously ringing, then cutting out after a set number of rings.

Once you have created a use case diagram describing the different functionalities that are needed, it then becomes possible to create an activity diagram for each of these use cases. The first two use cases are fairly straightforward and the activity diagrams may look something like this:

Fig. 47 - Example activity diagrams for receiving notification that a phone is engaged or disconnected:

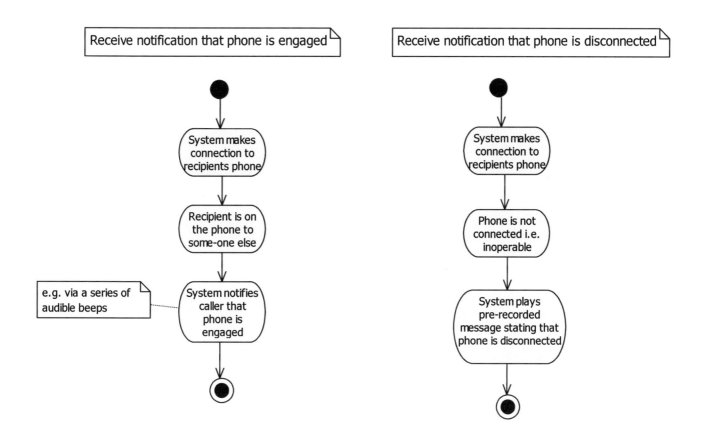

From the information in the diagrams shown in fig. 47, we can then create functional requirements that might look something like this:

Fig. 48 – Example functional requirements for receiving notification that a phone is disconnected or engaged:

Feature	ID	Requirement	Priority
Receive notification that phone is engaged	006	When recipient is already using the phone at time of call, system must notify phone user that phone is engaged (i.e. busy) Constraints: • Notification must take the form of a series of audible beeps • Notification must continue until phone user disconnects call	
Receive notification that phone is disconnected	007	If recipient's phone is disconnected (i.e. phone number is inoperable) system must notify phone user that the phone number is no longer in operation. Constraints: • Notification must take the form of an audible pre-recorded message • Pre-recorded message must state that phone number is no longer in operation	

Notice that in the above table I have added a column to the left called 'feature'. This very useful additional column enables the functional requirements to be traced back to the use cases (functionalities). If you want, you can add a fifth column to the table stating which user the requirement originated from.

The third use case – 'Receive notification that recipient is currently unavailable' is a little more complicated:

Fig. 49 – Example activity diagram for receiving notification that recipient is currently unavailable:

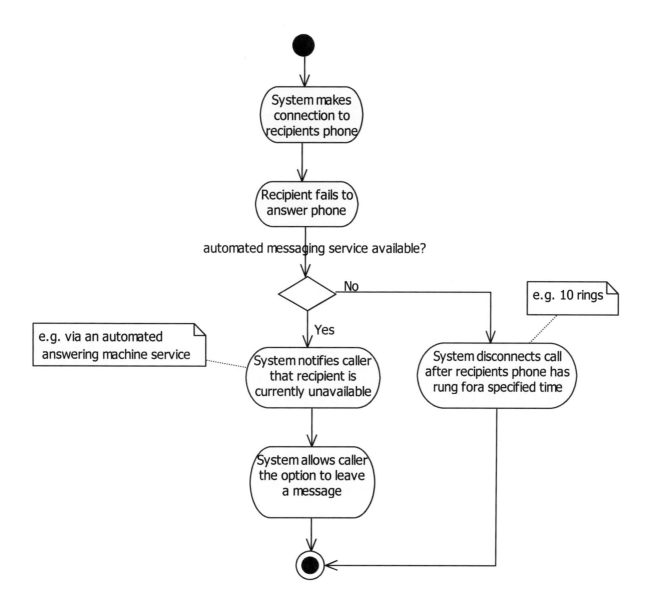

Again, we can turn these activities into functional requirements, add some constraints and the end result is a more detailed analysis of what needs to happen in this particular situation:

Fig. 50 – Example functional requirements for receiving notification that recipient is currently unavailable:

Feature	ID	Requirement	Priority
Receive notification that recipient is unavailable	008	When recipient fails to answer the phone and an automated messaging service is available, system must notify phone user that recipient is currently unavailable Constraints: • Notification must take the form of a pre-recorded message	
	009	When recipient fails to answer the phone and an automated messaging service is available, caller must have the ability to leave a message for the recipient	
	010	When recipient fails to answer the phone and an automated messaging service is not available, system must disconnect call after a specified number of rings Constraints: • Number of rings before call disconnects = 20	

Attributes - recording data requirements

We have now covered two of the three techniques for elaborating requirements. The last technique I want to discuss is used specifically to document 'data requirements' i.e. requirements that involve the use of data. To describe this third technique, I am going to use an example from the mathematical model activity diagrams, namely the example from Fig. 40 where a request for a parameter evaluation is being created:

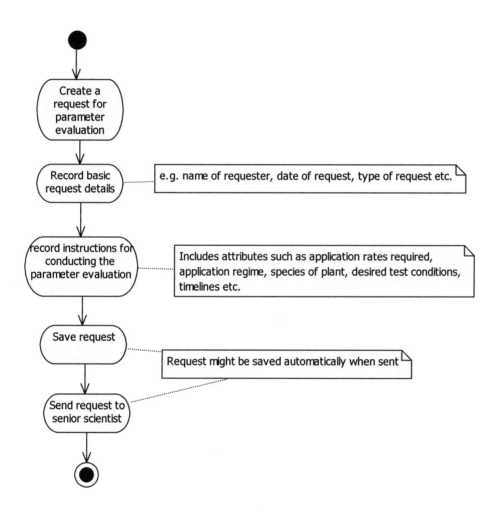

The second step shown in this activity diagram is 'record basic request details'. Now, if you turned this into a functional requirement it would probably read something like 'modeler needs the ability to record basic request details' or 'modeler must be able to record basic request details'. This isn't a particularly good requirement as the development team won't have a clue what these 'basic request details' are. So you are going to need to ask the users what information they want to record for this step, and document it.

This is where some of the work carried out on the concept diagram and competency questions comes in useful. If this had been a real situation, the concept diagram would have been updated when new concepts were identified during the creation of the use case diagram, activity diagrams and competency questions. The concept of a 'parameter evaluation request' might have been identified, along with some of its attributes. We do have a note associated with this activity step which lists some potential attributes:

- The name of a requester
- The date of the request
- The type of request

What we are seeing here is fundamentally a list of information, or 'data' that needs to be recorded. If we were to create a set of requirements to describe the recording of this data, the requirements might look something like this:

User needs the ability to record the name of a requester
User needs the ability to record the date of a request
User needs the ability to record the type of request
Etc.

Instead of creating a long list of 'data requirements', it is far better to record the list of attributes that are needed in a tabular format. This has several advantages:

- Listing the required attributes in a table makes it easier for people to see the complete list of attributes at a single glance
- It is very easy to associate additional information against each attribute, such as example values, whether the attribute is mandatory or optional etc.
- It allows the developer to clearly see which attributes are required for which purpose e.g. you can create a table of attributes needed for creating a request, another table for describing attributes needed for data capture, another table for describing which attributes will be used to conduct a search etc.
- It is very easy to associate a table of attributes (data) to a particular requirement e.g. by creating the table in an appendix and then referencing the appendix in the requirement

For example, if we were to create a table to describe the attributes needed for creating a parameter evaluation request, the table of information might look something like this:

Fig. 51 – List of attributes needed to create a parameter evaluation request:

Attributes	Example value	Format	Mandatory?	Constraints and notes
ID	PER01	Alphanumeric	Y	Auto generated by system
Name of requester	Martin White	Alphanumeric	Y	Must include first name and last name
Date of request	17-Aug-2016	Date	Y	Date format = DD-MMM-YYYY
Type of Request	Field evaluation	Alphanumeric	Y	
Etc.				

There is now a significant amount of information available for each attribute that is needed. I would recommend that you include in your table, the following information against each attribute (as a minimum):

- The name of the attribute
- an example value for each attribute
- The data format for the attribute, e.g. will the value for the attribute be a numerical value? Or a text (alphanumerical) value? Does it need to be a date?
- Whether the attribute is mandatory or optional i.e. does a value always need to be recorded against the attribute or is this optional?
- Any constraints and notes. You can use this column in your table to describe any system rules as well (we will come on to this later in chapter 16).

You may also want to record additional information such as the number of characters required for each attribute.

Once you have a table describing the list of attributes needed for a particular requirement, you will need to create an appendix for the table in the requirements specification document and reference the appendix from the requirement e.g.

'Modeler needs the ability to record the basic request details described in Appendix 1'

Creating a list of attributes in a tabular format and referencing the table from a requirement is extremely useful in cases where the users need to record something, change something, view something, search for something, generate reports etc. In fact, any situation where there is information or data involved. There will be some cases where you can reference the same table from multiple requirements, but it is far more likely that you will need to create several of these attribute tables and therefore several appendices – one for each table. Keeping the tables of attributes updated during the development phase is absolutely crucial. The column describing the constraints and notes is also ideal for recording rules, formulae for calculations and any other information that could be useful to the development team.

Documenting functional requirements in the form of user stories

You could if you wish, document your functional requirements as user stories and acceptance criteria instead of simple requirement statements. Now, let's think about this for a moment. The approach described in this book is based on three things: process, functionality and concepts. Where business requirements equate to functionality and must be written in an unambiguous single line statement, user stories relate to a user doing something that provides value to that user and it is possible for these to be written in a more ambiguous fashion. The ambiguity is usually resolved in a series of meetings with users to flesh out the detail of the user story. The detail is written as acceptance criteria, which in theory equates loosely to the functional requirements. Acceptance criteria is actually a set of conditions that need to be satisfied (and accepted) for a particular user story. The acceptance criteria describe the tests that need to be carried out to confirm that a user story is complete and working as intended. So acceptance criteria do relate to the functional requirements in that they effectively include the functional requirements in the form of a measure of what the functional requirement is meant to do. However, acceptance criteria only describe the requirements that are needed to satisfy a particular user story. If there are additional requirements that are 'nice to have' but are not a condition for acceptance of a user story, these requirements will probably not be included within the acceptance criteria.

Now, using the approach described in this book, we are not trying to flesh out detail from ambiguity; we are fleshing out detail from structured process. Is it possible to create user stories and acceptance criteria using this approach in the same way that we created simple requirements statements with constraints and tables of attributes? Yes, I can see no reason why you cannot do this. In fact there are two distinct benefits to using this approach for describing user stories and acceptance criteria. Firstly, you will be using a process driven structured approach that is designed to minimize ambiguity – your user stories can be written in an unambiguous way as you will have a clearer idea about the functionality that is required (as it is already described in the use case diagrams). Secondly, you will effectively be mapping your user stories and acceptance criteria to the 'To Be' process and activity diagrams. This overcomes one of the deficiencies of user stories – the lack of direct relationship to the business process.

In chapter 11 we saw how it was possible to create a set of user stories based on the functionalities (or use cases). A user story can generally be equated to a business requirement. In the same way, we could use the activity steps within the use case to describe a list of the acceptance criteria instead of a list of functional requirement statements. Or in other words, an acceptance criteria can generally be equated to a functional requirement.

Let's take the simple example of making a phone call. Described as a use case, the use case would be 'make phone call'. The business requirement might be 'phone user needs the ability to make a phone call'. If we described this as a user story instead of a business requirement we might end up with something like this:

'As a phone user, I want to make a phone call in order to communicate with my friends'.

Let's take another look at the activity diagram described in fig. 43 which describes the process for making a phone call:

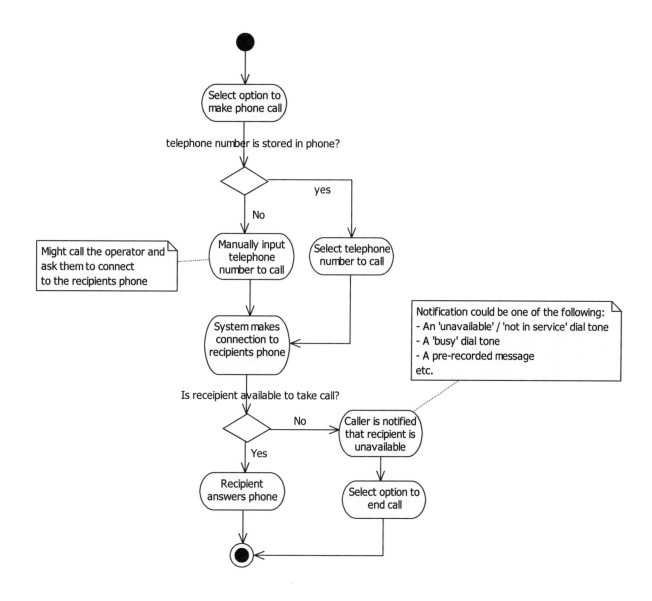

Now, we can use this activity diagram to document each of the activity steps as acceptance criteria e.g.

A phone user must be able to make a phone call
A phone user must be able to manually input a telephone number to call
A phone user must be able to select a telephone number to call
The phone makes a connection to the recipients phone
The phone user is notified if the recipient is unavailable
The call is ended when the phone user disconnects from the call

So far so good. What happens though when we want to document the constraints that were identified? Well, these can be added to the list as additional acceptance criteria. What about the data requirements i.e. the list of attributes? Again, we can refer to the tables in the appendices in the same manner as we did with the functional requirement statement, or alternatively we would need to document each attribute in the form of acceptance criteria, but this would be a bit long winded…

So yes, it is possible to create user stories with acceptance criteria using this approach. In fact, following this approach should help resolve the ambiguity of high level user stories and enable the definition of structured acceptance criteria for the user stories. However, when working in an iterative fashion on a project (time-boxed or not) that does not necessitate the use of user stories then personally I would use functional requirement statements and constraints in preference to user stories. This is just personal preference though. At the end of the day, you will need to choose whatever works best for you and achieves the desired goal i.e. a defined list of functional requirements that are clear, testable and most importantly, correct.

Requirements Traceability

From Wikipedia: 'Traceability is the ability to verify the history, location, or application of an item by means of documented recorded identification'. Requirements traceability is all about being able to view the life of a requirement in terms of what it is associated with and where it came from.

Using the approach described in this book, a functional requirement can be viewed as being directly related to a business requirement in the same way that an activity step is directly related to a use case. Because a use case is also directly related to a process step, there is traceability from functional requirements to business requirements, through to process. There is also traceability from functional requirements through to concepts by way of the attribute tables. Where traceability really becomes important though, is when the development team starts to test the solution to determine if the requirements have been met. The writing of test cases or validation criteria to assess the solution is outside the scope of this book; it is usually (but not always!) an activity carried out by a test team and should not be the responsibility of the business analyst. Tracing a functional requirement (or a non-functional requirement) to a test case is very important – how else will the team know that the requirements have been properly met?

There are tools available to manage the traceability of one requirement to another and the traceability of requirements to test cases. Usually an analyst would create a traceability matrix for the purpose of determining if making a change to one requirement might have an impact on another requirement, but using the approach outlined in this book this should not be necessary. By changing a requirement you are effectively changing a step in a process, so the impact of a change would be obvious at the process level i.e. shown in the activity diagrams. If you change a functional requirement you will need to change the equivalent step in the activity diagram and vice versa.

So in general, the only traceability that you really need to worry about is that from the requirements to the test cases and if you are lucky, you can let the test team handle this.

Requirements Management

The documenting, editing, prioritizing, sharing and the managing of changes to requirements is known as 'requirements management'. Many analysts use specific requirement management tools to manage their requirements, because depending on how much 'managing' is being conducted, it can be a complicated process. Up until this point, I have only mentioned documenting requirements using a requirements specification template. However, depending on what type of project you are working on, there will probably come a point in time where maintaining a list of requirements in a single document may not be practical or even feasible.

Any requirements that you have written will need to be shared with stakeholders, vendors and the development team. The requirements specification document provides a convenient package of information that can be easily shared and communicated, **but only up to the point that work on the solution begins**. Once this point is reached and a vendor or development team is involved, additional factors come into play that make managing requirements in a single document much harder to accomplish.

What sort of additional factors come into play? Well, let's list out a few of the things that can happen to your requirements at this stage:

- The requirements will probably need to be prioritized by the development team and 'time boxed' i.e. the team will need to agree on the timing and order in which requirements / user stories will be tackled.
- If you are following an 'agile' development methodology then there will probably be a 'backlog' (to do list) of requirements / user stories that needs to be maintained. This 'backlog' needs to be communicated and updated as the project progresses.
- Additional detail or clarity might be required and this will need to be added to your requirements.
- Changes / amendments to your requirements might need to be made. These have to be made visible to all interested parties.
- If things change, it is useful to keep a record of what has changed and why.

For the above reasons, and many more, it may not be practical to maintain your requirements in a requirements specification document. You (and the development team) may need a requirements management tool to manage any changes, prioritization and status tracking of your requirements.

I would suggest that once you reach that point in time where a development team or vendor is actively involved in creating the solution, the requirements that you have documented in the specification document are copied across to a suitable requirements management tool. You no longer update the requirements in the specification document; instead you (or the development team) maintain them in the requirements management tool.

The tool should provide an identifier for each requirement / user story, which can be used as a reference. You will need to copy this reference identifier across to your requirements specification document.

Why not just abandon the requirements specification document at this stage? Do we even still need it? Yes, we most certainly do. As stated earlier, if a requirement changes then it will affect the workflow that has been documented. Each step in a workflow equates to a functional requirement (or in terms of a user story, an acceptance criteria). So if there is a change to a requirement, there will also be a change to the workflow in an activity diagram. The diagram will need to be updated and made visible to the stakeholders. By documenting and communicating a workflow or process change, you are also effectively assessing the impact of that change to the users.

Although requirement management tools are ideal for managing requirements, they are generally not so good at handling diagrams. There are exceptions of course; some tools have been designed so that all the diagramming and requirements documentation can be conducted within the one tool or suite of tools e.g. the toolset that Blueprint Software Systems provides. However, unless you are actively using a tool that can handle both diagrams and requirements, you will still need a requirements specification document to be able to communicate changes to the diagrams and to serve as a convenient summary of information about the work.

Summary

In summary, a list of functional requirements can be obtained directly from the activity diagrams and documented initially within a requirements specification document. Certain techniques can be used to flesh out the detail of the requirements including documenting constraints, breaking down complicated requirements into more granular requirements and creating tabulated lists of attributes that can be referenced by the requirements.

Once development work begins in earnest, requirements should then be copied or transferred to a requirements management tool so that any changes to the requirements can be properly and effectively managed. This also applies to non-functional requirements as well, which we will take a look at in the next chapter.

Chapter 15 – Define the Non-Functional Requirements

We now come to something that is always a bit of a challenge for the business analyst – the defining of non-functional requirements. Whereas a functional requirement describes how the solution needs to operate functionally i.e. what the solution is meant to do, a non-functional requirement describes the quality and the aesthetics of the solution i.e. what the solution is meant to 'be'. Non-functional requirements describe how the solution needs to perform, how efficient it needs to be, how accessible it needs to be, what its dependencies are on other things, what the legal or licensing ramifications are, how it needs to be deployed etc. Because some of these requirements are somewhat intangible in terms of properties, there is often great difficulty in specifying what it is the development team need to deliver in terms of the non-functional requirements.

These non-functional requirements are also extremely important. From a user's viewpoint, the development team can deliver a solution that meets all of the functional requirements, but if it doesn't meet the non-functional requirements the stakeholders won't use it. The solution will be effectively useless. From an architectural viewpoint, without the non-functional requirements it would very difficult if not impossible to deliver a properly functioning solution.

Ironically, non-functional requirements (from the user's viewpoint) are the simplest of requirements to define:

The system must be fast. It must be easy to use. It must be intuitive. It must have a high quality look and feel. It must be responsive etc.

These are all non-functional requirements and if you gave them to a developer or test team they would throw up their hands in horror and send you away with a flea in your ear. The most important thing about defining non-functional requirements properly is that they need to be measurable.

How do you measure something as intangible as 'easy to use'? Or 'high quality look and feel'? The answer is… it's not easy. You can however measure things like performance, availability, reliability and compliance. You can use response times to measure performance. You can measure the mean time between failures to measure reliability. You can state at what times the solution needs to be available and you can define what the solution needs to be compliant with. There are distinct ways to include measurements in the non-functional requirements and many of these non-functional requirements can then be re-used. Here is a list of the top ten features (in no particular order) that you would need to think about when defining non-functional requirements:

1. Performance (efficiency)
2. Availability
3. Maintainability (support, deployment)
4. Reliability (robustness, stability)
5. Compliance
6. Accessibility (Security)
7. Dependency

8. Compatibility
9. Legal & licensing
10. Usability (complexity, look and feel)

You can also add 'price' to this list as it's often one of the most important factors when considering a solution, but because this is something that is relatively easy to quantify, I've left it out of the top ten.

The best way of illustrating how to write non-functional requirements is to use an example, and Joe Bloggs with his ever present phone problem is nicely on hand to oblige…

When you talk about non-functional requirements with a stakeholder, you need to get to the measurements for the requirement just as you need to get to the root cause of the problem when you talk about the problem. When we tried to get to the root cause of the problem, we asked the question 'why?' i.e. why is this a problem? With non-functional requirements, instead of asking the question 'why', you will need to ask the question 'how'. How would you measure this?

If you went through the above top ten list of non-functional features with Joe Bloggs in relation to the new phone that he's after and asked the question 'how would you measure this?' against each item, you would possibly end up with something like this (not a comprehensive list!):

Fig. 52 – example list of non-functional requirements for the phone problem

Feature	ID	Requirement	Priority
Performance	NF01	When switching on the phone, the phone must allow access to all functionality within 2 seconds	High
	NF02	When sending a text message, the phone must send the message to the recipient within 2 seconds	High
	NF03	When making a phone call, the phone must connect to the recipient within 2 seconds	High
	NF04	When selecting to view an image on the phone, the image must be displayed on the screen within 1 second	Medium
Availability	NF05	The phone must be available for use 24 hours a day, 7 days a week.	High
Maintainability	NF06	If the phone develops a fault, it must be possible for the phone to be repaired within 24 hours.	Medium
Reliability	NF07	The phone must be able to operate for at least two years without developing a fault.	High
Compliance	NF08	The phone must be compliant with both SMS and MMS messaging services	High
Accessibility	NF09	It must be possible to protect the phone from unauthorized access e.g. by using a password or fingerprint recognition system	High
	NF10	Only the phone user can have authorized access to the phone at any one time.	High
Dependency	NF11	The phone must be able to access an 'App store' in order to download games and other content	High
Compatibility	NF12	The phone must be compatible with any PAYG service provider	High
	NF13	The phone must be able to operate in any country in the world	Medium
Legal & licensing	NF14	The phone must comply with Ofcom licensing standards	Medium
Usability	NF15	The phone must have a screen size of no more than 12cm	High
	NF16	The phone must have a screen resolution of 1920 x 1080 pixels	Medium
	NF17	The phone must be black	Medium
	NF18	The phone must provide a user interface that uses symbols and icons that are easily recognized by 80% of the target stakeholders	High
	NF19	It must be possible for 80% of the stakeholders to use the phone without having to refer to an instruction manual	High

Let's quickly go through the above to clarify a few points:

Performance – how well (or efficiently) a piece of work, task or function is carried out. This is something that can be measured, usually in terms of speed. So the question to ask here is… how fast is fast? Under what circumstances do you need performance? Different operations may require different performance. Obviously you don't want to list out every operation and how quickly that operation needs to be performed, but you do need to list out some of the key ones.

Availability – how obtainable or accessible something is. Be careful with this one. There is usually a cost associated with making something available for extended periods of time, especially if that availability involves some form of maintenance or support. There is also the question of time zones – if you specify that something needs to be available between the hours of 9.00 a.m. and 5.00 p.m., you may also need to specify which time zone you are talking about. 9.00 a.m. in the USA will not be 9.00 a.m. in Europe or Asia.

Maintainability - keeping something operating and functional. This can also include any specific requirements for support and deployment of the solution. Things like maintaining the synchronization of data between multiple servers in different parts of the world might come under this heading, although the ability to synchronize data between two or more data sources will be a functional requirement. As you go through the non-functional requirements you may well start to identify additional functional requirements that will need to be added (to your functional requirements). Administration of data and system security permissions are two areas where it is highly likely that additional functional requirements will need to be defined.

Reliability – the extent to which something can be relied or depended upon. This is one of those intangible things that can be difficult to measure properly. You can ask for something to be reliable in the sense that it should work without any faults for at least a defined number of years. There is of course, no guarantee that it will work for that number of years, or months. It might suddenly and inexplicably fail within 24 hours. This is a difficult requirement to test…

Compliance – the act of complying with or obeying a wish or command. You should be able to state quite clearly what the solution needs to be compliant with (if anything). There are often regulations and guidelines specifying numerous rules that must be adhered to… if any of this is relevant then just reference it in the requirements.

Accessibility – By this I mean access to the solution. You will need to include the number of stakeholders that need to access the system in this section, as well how many need access to the solution at the same time. When we talk about access to something, the issue of security and roles invariably crops up. Suffice it to say that you can cover the requirements for system roles and security by defining them as either functional requirements, non-functional requirements, business rules, or a mixture of all three. As long as you have this area covered and the development team knows what is required in terms of security and access to the system, it doesn't really matter where you define them.

Dependency – the relationship between two or more things which involves one being dependant on another in order to operate effectively. The solution may well be dependent on other systems or processes. This should be fairly straightforward to define, as long as your stakeholders (or architects) know what the dependencies are.

Compatibility – a state where two or more things can exist together without problems or conflict. Again, this should be fairly straightforward to define if you list the things that the solution needs to be compatible with. If the solution needs to be compatible with e.g. a particular operating system or way of working, you can state that in this section.

Legal & licensing – this is different from compliance in that what you are stating here is any specific legal or licensing issues e.g. if the solution involves the need for stakeholders to purchase a license to use it, how many licenses would be needed, any issues around patents etc.

Usability – this is the tough one. Usability includes the look and feel of the solution, how easy it is to use etc. You cannot easily measure these properties, so you have to define the things that make the solution easy to use or that provide the look and feel that makes the solution desirable. What is it that the users really want here? You may have to ask a lot of questions to get to the root of what will make the solution 'look and feel right'. In terms of complexity or ease of use, it is possible to provide a very generic sort of measure for this, but again it is not very easily testable. In the example above we have stated that 80% of the stakeholders using the solution must be satisfied with the icons and symbols used in the user interface or be able to use the solution without having to refer to a set of instructions. In the particular example where there is only one user, Joe Bloggs, this is pretty easy to test. Not so easy if you have several thousand stakeholders from all over the world using the solution, but it is possible (e.g. by sending out a survey).

In summary, non –functional requirements cannot be derived from the process in the same way that we can derive functional requirements. There is no short cut route to defining non-functional requirements; you will need to spend a session with the users and subject matter experts to define these. However, you will find that the session can be made more painless by re-using non-functional requirements that have already been defined (e.g. from other projects) and adapting them to your user's needs. You may also find that non-functional requirements start appearing as you discuss the detailed 'To Be' process with the users during the creation of the activity diagrams. As you discuss the process and functionality required with the users, you may well come across non-functional requirements, especially when the future process is addressing a particular problem (or 'pain point').

Chapter 16 – Define the Business (and System) Rules

We are now at the last activity shown in the approach, but you do not necessarily have to wait until this point to have started defining the business rules. In fact, it is highly likely that during conversations with your stakeholders when discussing the process and activity diagrams, the concept diagrams and most especially the functional requirements, you will have already begun to define some 'business rules'. A business rule is basically a rule that defines or limits some aspect regarding the business. A business rule is a type of constraint, but it is not a constraint specific to a particular requirement. In chapter 14 we discussed documenting constraints against requirements where the constraint was a limitation or restriction regarding the requirement. A business rule however, is a constraint that applies to either a business concept, a process or a step in the process. It is a 'higher level' constraint than those documented at the functional requirement level.

You may have also heard the term 'system rule'. A system rule defines or limits some aspect regarding the 'system'. System rules are of particular interest to the development team and system rules are most often associated with attributes. We will take a look at both business and system rules in this chapter.

Let's start from the top… you are most likely to actively come across business rules when defining the 'To Be' process. However, there may already be business rules occurring within the 'As Is' process that can potentially be re-used. You will need to check with the users if existing business rules are still relevant and likely to be part of, or have a direct impact on, the 'To Be' process.

Now, how do you actually find these business rules? Well, business rules can occur most prominently under certain situations and the most common situations are (in no particular order):

- Progression – when something is progressed from one state to another
- Security access - when someone wants to access a system
- Security permission - when someone needs to have the correct permission (access rights) to carry out a process
- Policies – when certain policies, conditions or standard operating procedures need to be adhered to
- Calculations – when something needs to be calculated
- Storage and archiving – when something needs to be stored
- Creation and deletion – when something needs to be created or removed

The above is not a comprehensive list!

The following business process diagram could in theory, contain many business rules:

Fig. 53 – Process for making changes to a website:

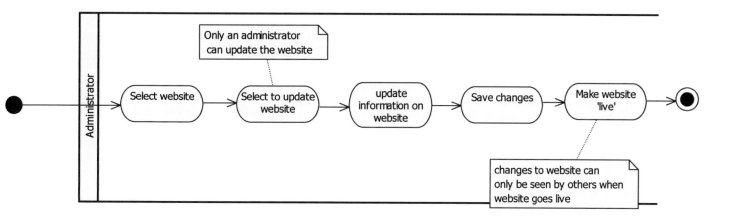

Using the above diagram as an example, there may be one or more business rules related to accessing the system (in this case the website administration system) e.g.

- The administrator must have a valid license in order to use the website administration software

When the website is updated, the following business rules may come into effect regarding access permissions e.g.:

- Only an administrator can make changes to a website
- The administrator cannot change the style of the website, only the content

When the website is saved, there may be a business rule stating e.g.:

- No-one else apart from the administrator can view the saved changes to the website until the website goes live

When the website is made live, there may be a business rule stating e.g.:

- The status of the website must be changed from 'draft' to 'live' before anyone else apart from the administrator can view changes to the website

The example above relates to business rules at the process level and these are the sort of business rules that can be added as a list to your requirements specification document in a section called 'business rules'. You can categorize these business rules by process and just list them in the business rules section – not a problem. They become a high level, pretty straightforward set of business rules.

You may also find business rules when discussing activities or functional requirements. Let's take an example:

Joe Bloggs wants to play his 'kill the zombies' video game. When he achieves a particular best score, he wants that score to be displayed on two high score tables, one showing his personal best scores (a 'local' high score table) and the other showing his score in relation to other players who also play the game (a 'global' high score table). He doesn't want other players to be able to view his own local high score table. He doesn't want to see the other players' local high score tables either. This example isn't really connected to Joe's phone problem because it's the game itself that will need to display the high score information, so this example is describing something that in reality would be out of scope. But let's ignore that fact for now and carry on with the example anyway! How do we define all this in terms of the requirements and business rules?

Let's start with the process first:

Fig. 54 – Activity diagram showing the process for updating a high score:

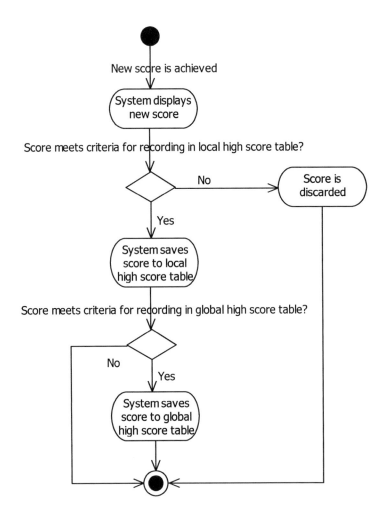

So in terms of process, Joe Bloggs plays his game and obtains a new score. He can view the score and if it meets the criteria for making the local high score table, the score will be added to this table.

If the score meets the criteria for making the global high score table, then the score will be also be added to that table.

Viewing the high score tables would be another (different) piece of functionality; we are only concerned with *updating* the high score here, so there's nothing included in this process about viewing high score tables. So far so good... we have a basic process but we haven't defined any criteria for recording high scores in either table. Nor have we mentioned anything about who can or can't view the high score tables. Let's move on – we can write out some functional requirements:

Fig. 55 – Requirements for updating a high score:

Feature	ID	Requirement	Priority
Update high score table .	01	When a new score is achieved, system must display the new score	High
	02	If new score meets the criteria for inclusion in the local high score table, system must save the score to the local high score table.	High
	03	If new score does not meet the criteria for inclusion in the local high score table, system must discard the score i.e. score is not saved anywhere.	High
	04	If new score meets the criteria for inclusion in the global high score table, system must save the score to the global high score table.	High

Now, at this point we could potentially speak to the stakeholders and ask some probing questions to work out what the business rules would be. As soon as you see something in the requirements that states something vague like 'meeting the criteria' or 'achieving a particular value' or 'once it gets to a certain stage' then you know there must be some underlying rules that will define what the criteria are, or how you get to the particular value or how you get to that 'certain stage'... you have ambiguity in your requirements and you can either resolve it on the spot or just move on and tackle it later, probably when you're working with the development team during the iterative development of the solution.

For this example though, let's imagine that we are delving into the detail right now and extracting a set of business rules from the minds of the stakeholders. We need to know what defines the criteria for making it onto the high score tables. What are the rules that state whether a player has made it onto these tables or not? Let's make some stuff up...

- Only the 10 best scores will make it onto the local high score table.
- The score has to be greater than the lowest score already on the (local high score table
- No-one else can view a players local (personal) high score table

And so on... usually you should be able to come up with a pretty comprehensive set of business rules by talking to the stakeholders.

Now I said earlier that a business rule is a constraint that is applied against a process, a concept or an activity, but not against a specific requirement. Does this actually hold true though? Where you have business rules that could be associated with a requirement, there will be a strong temptation to record these business rules as constraints directly against the requirement. I will describe why this is not such a great idea in a minute… for now let's just see what it looks like (with the addition of some more potential business rules):

Fig. 56 – Requirements for updating a high score, including constraints:

Feature	ID	Requirement	Priority
Update high score table	01	When a new score is achieved, system must display the new score	High
	02	If new score meets the criteria for inclusion in the local high score table, system must save the score to the local high score table. Constraints: • Local high score table must only include the ten best scores • A new score can only be included in local high score table if score is greater than the lowest score in the table. • A local high score table must belong solely to an individual player • No other player can view the scores in a local high score table that does not belong to that player	High
	03	If new score does not meet the criteria for inclusion in the local high score table, system must discard the score i.e. score is not saved anywhere.	High
	04	If new score meets the criteria for inclusion in the global high score table, system must save the score to the global high score table. Constraints: • If a score for the player does not already exist in the global high score table, the score must be added to the table • If the new score is higher than the score already recorded for that player in the global high score table, the new score must overwrite the old score in the global high score table. • If the new score is lower than the score already recorded for that player in the global high score table, no changes are made to the score already recorded in the global high score table. • All players of the game can view the scores in the global high score table.	High

Looking at the above, you might notice something that isn't immediately obvious. These business rules are not necessarily going to be specific to the requirements they are written against; they might also be relevant to other requirements describing operations using a local or global high score table. For example, the business rule stating 'No other player can view the scores in a local high score table that does not belong to that player' could also be relevant for requirements around security access and viewing of high scores. In fact, a business rule is not associated with a requirement in the same way that a business rule is associated with a process step. A business rule at this level of detail is generally associated with a *concept*. In fig. 56 we are really talking about requirements based on two concepts – a local high score table and a global high score table. The business rules are not really specific to the requirements we have listed; they are however specific to the concepts. We have a concept of a 'local high score table' and that list of business rules in requirement 02 relates directly to that concept, just as the list of business rules in requirement 04 relates directly to the concept of a 'global high score table'. So listing the business rules against specific requirements as 'constraints' is not a good idea. Where then is the best place to document business rules?

Documenting business rules

Listing some business rules against processes and others against requirements can be very problematic. Firstly, your business rules will end up all over the place. Some will be at the process level in a separate business rules section and others will be scattered throughout the functional requirements and mixed in with the constraints. It becomes messy and could end up being difficult to manage, especially if you have a lot of business rules. The most efficient way to document the business rules is to put them all in one place in the document under a section titled 'business rules'. They can then be categorized as being business rules relating to either a process / workflow step or a concept and each rule given a unique identifier. The main benefit here is that they are all in one place and easy to view. It would look something like this:

Fig. 57 - List of Business Rules

Business Rules:

Process:

Process step	ID	Business Rule
Access system	BR01	The administrator must have a valid license in order to use the website administration software
Update Website	BR02	Only an administrator can make changes to a website
	BR03	The administrator cannot change the style of the website, only the content

Concepts:

Concept	ID	Business Rule
Local high score table	BR04	Local high score table must only include the ten best scores
	BR05	A new score can only be included in local high score table if score is greater than the lowest score in the table.
	BR06	A local high score table must belong solely to an individual player
Global high score table	BR07	If a score for the player does not already exist in the global high score table, the score must be added to the table
	BR08	If the new score is higher than the score already recorded for that player in the global high score table, the new score must overwrite the old score in the global high score table.
	BR09	If the new score is lower than the score already recorded for that player in the global high score table, no changes are made to the score already recorded in the global high score table.

Business rule conditions

The more detailed you get with the requirements, the more likely you are to come across circumstances where 'conditions' are introduced. By the term 'condition', I mean that the particular state an object is in at any one point in time may have a bearing or create a dependency on something else. Or in other words, you have a business rule that states something like... 'IF (or WHEN) 'X' happens, then 'Y' must happen. As soon as you introduce the words 'if' or 'when' into the mix, you will introduce a condition into the business rule and as a consequence, potentially some complexity.

We have already documented some business rules (above) where the word 'If' creates a condition in the rule. These are very simple rules though… you might end up with a complicated business rule that states something like:

'If both 'X' and 'Y' happen at the same time, or if 'A' and 'B' happen at the same time, then 'C' must overwrite 'D' unless 'X' is greater than 70%'.

The important thing here is to make sure that the business rule reads as a logical statement and that it is correct. If you are lucky you can try to break the rule down into simpler statements but this is not always possible. You can also try to illustrate complicated business rules using a 'mock-up' - we will come on to mock-up's in the next chapter. By the way, the use of conditions in a rule also applies equally to system rules; system rules may also contain conditions…

System rules

The difference between a system rule and a business rule can sometimes appear quite subtle. A system rule defines or limits some aspect regarding the 'system', but many business rules also do the same. In the examples above, we have business rules that apply to high score tables in a 'system'. What makes these rules 'business rules' and not 'system rules'?

The main thing that makes these 'business rules' is that they relate to either a process, which is an operation or activity carried out by the business, or they relate to a concept, which is a 'thing' of interest to the business. Whereas a system rule relates either directly to the system itself in terms of infrastructure or software, or to the data stored in the system. With regards the system itself, it is not your job to define the system rules. You as an analyst need to concentrate on defining the elements that will enable a solution to be chosen or developed; it is really the development teams' responsibility to define any system rules relating to potential system infrastructure. Having said that, you as an analyst may well identify and define system rules at the data (attribute) level.

Let's take a quick step back. When identifying business rules you will be looking first at process diagrams, then at activity diagrams, then at functional requirements and ultimately at concepts. There is one level of detail below concepts and that is 'attributes'. It is at this level of detail where you are most likely to find important system rules, because in terms of a 'system', the attributes that you have described as being necessary for certain functional requirements are more than likely going to be synonymous with the data stored in the system.

Let's take another look at the example list of attributes we defined back in chapter 14 from Fig. 51:

Attributes	Example value	Format	Mandatory?	Constraints and notes
ID	PER01	Alphanumeric	Y	Auto generated by system
Name of requester	Martin White	Alphanumeric	Y	Must include first name and last name
Date of request	17-Aug-2016	Date	Y	Date format = DD-MMM-YYYY
Type of Request	Field evaluation	Alphanumeric	Y	

There are some example constraints listed against these attributes. The constraints recorded against these attributes can all be regarded as system (or data) rules because these are rules that relate directly to the attributes i.e. the data.

I would strongly recommend that once you get down to the level of the attributes, you keep these system rules in the tables in the 'notes and constraints' column. You do not need a section in your requirements specification document titled 'system rules'. If you did pull all of the system rules out into a separate section of your requirements specification document you will actually make it harder for the development team to understand, because the other information in the attribute table complements the system rules and puts them into context, especially regarding the example values (which must follow the system rules!). The developer would need to reference both sets of information in order to view the attributes properly in context. Documenting the system rules as constraints against the attributes (data) makes it very clear to the development team what the rules are for each data attribute.

Chapter 17 – Other Useful Techniques – 'Mock-ups' and SWOT Analysis

We have now covered each of the elements of the approach described in the process diagram in fig. 1! If you have successfully used the approach and applied the techniques described in this book to your project, you should by now (if not sooner) have reached the point where there is sufficient information available to a development team to begin work on the solution. This is not to say that your job ends here… you will still be required to support the development of the solution, probably by fleshing out more detail on the requirements or process, maybe by helping answer particular questions from the development team relating to the requirements etc. If you are following my suggested ways of working then you will be involved in an iterative development approach, where work is probably (but not necessarily) time-boxed, maybe by using the use cases to time-box the development. Or you may be using one of the agile methodologies and have created a set of user stories in place of the business and functional requirements.

Either way, although we have covered the basics of the approach (hopefully in sufficient detail for you to use), there are a couple of other useful techniques which might prove of benefit at any point when working through this approach:

Mock-ups

A 'mock-up' is basically a model, used to enhance or generate understanding of something. It differs from a 'prototype' in that a mock-up is a static or fixed model that doesn't provide any working functionality, whereas a prototype is a dynamic model that does provide some working functionality.

A mock-up can be created using any tool you like. It can be as simple as a diagram created on a piece of paper, or it can be as complicated as a scale model made with Lego bricks or balsa wood. There are several freeware tools available that are suitable for creating mock-ups. Tools such as Microsoft PowerPoint, Visio and Excel can also be used to create mock-ups.

Mock-up's can be very useful to help determine what information is required (in terms of both input and output) or to help describe what something should look like. For example, we could create a mock-up showing what the output of a report might look like, or what information needs to be displayed when inputting data, or what information needs to be displayed when adhering to one or more very complicated business or system rules. The key thing to note with using mock-ups for analysis is that you are not trying to design anything… you are not a designer or an architect. You should be concerning yourself with just modeling functionality. So don't make your mock-ups too elaborate, keep them simple and easily understandable.

An example mock-up:

Fig. 58 – example mockup showing input screen for a 'parameter evaluation request':

Request for Parameter Evaluation

Name of requester	Matt / Simon

Date of request	28 Mar 2016	Date needed by:	14 July 2016

Type of request	Field Evaluation

Instructions:

Application Rates:	5 ppm, 10 ppm, 20 ppm

Application regime:	Spray twice a week

Species	Cotton / Corn

Test conditions	text

Submit

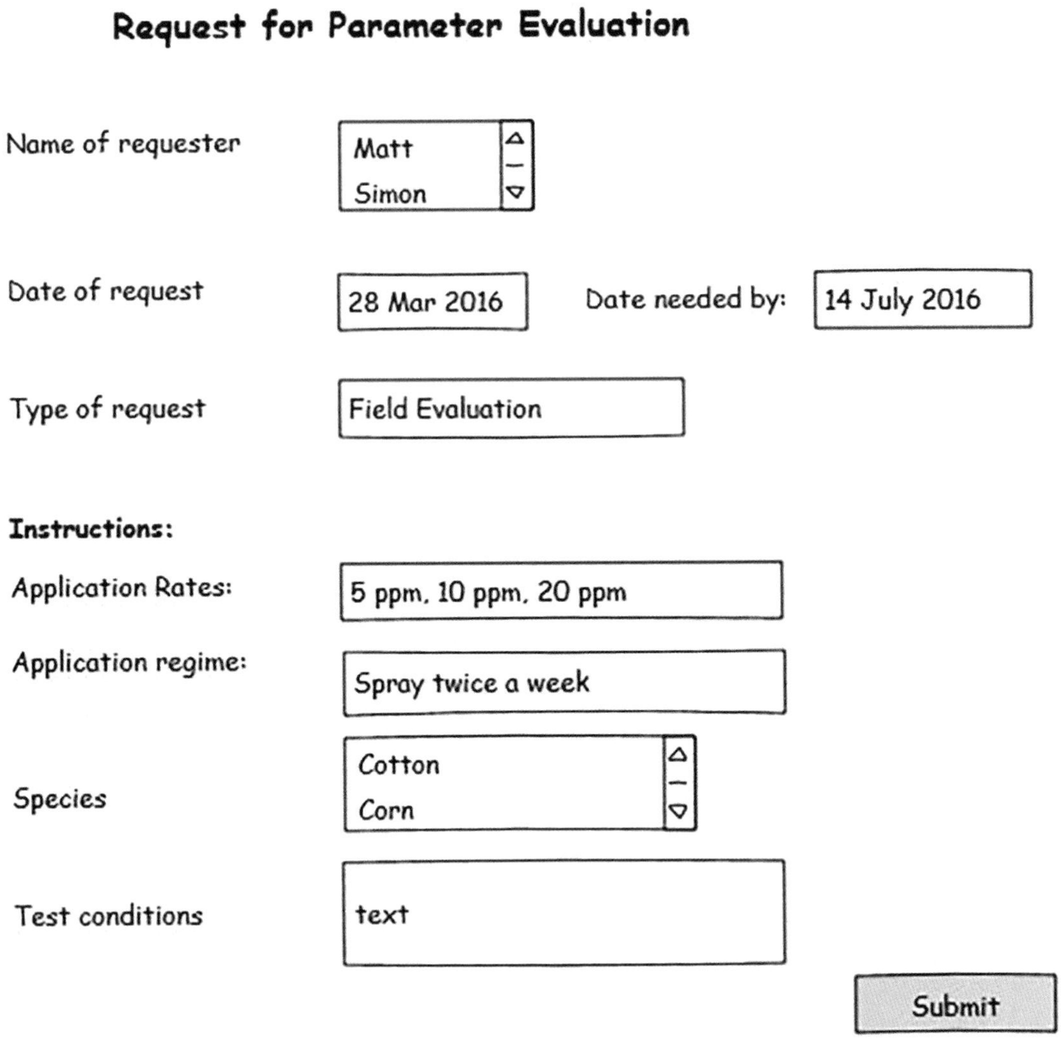

The mock-up above represents a model showing what a 'parameter evaluation request' might look like, in terms of the user interface. The mockup shows simple labels and boxes; it could represent a vision for how the request form should appear to a modeler, in terms of the fields required and the rough layout of those fields. Something like this can be quick and easy to create; it conveys a simple message and it doesn't attempt to emulate a proper graphical user interface in appearance. The disadvantage of making a mock-up appear too 'pretty' is that the stakeholders may get the impression that what you have drawn is precisely what they will get. This is also a potential problem with using prototypes; it is easy to raise false expectations when showing people a model, especially a working model. It may not actually be possible to develop the solution to look exactly like the model…

In situations such as describing how something should be displayed, it is far easier (and often clearer) to create a mock-up than it is to write out a list of textual requirements. When documenting requirements for user interfaces, I would suggest creating one or more mock-ups to accompany the functional requirements.

A mock-up can prove useful, especially when trying to describe something complicated or to gain a better understanding of what a user wants to do. Having the user create the mock-up can also prove extremely useful!

SWOT Analysis

'SWOT' is an acronym for 'Strengths, Weaknesses, Opportunities and Threats'. It is usually represented as a matrix table – two columns and two rows – like this:

Strengths	Weaknesses
Opportunities	Threats

A SWOT analysis is the work required to fill in the table with something meaningful; it is a way of weighing up the pros and cons in a logical comparative fashion. A SWOT analysis is often carried out when the users are faced with a difficult decision to make that involves choosing between multiple solution options. For example there might be a question regarding which tool to purchase or which vendor to go with… answering these types of question can be difficult without some means of logical analysis. You would need to create a SWOT analysis table for each option, then review the SWOT analysis tables with the stakeholders (including the development team). You can start filling in the columns for each table with your own thoughts initially, then add to the tables during the review with the stakeholders. Or if you prefer, set up a dedicated session with the stakeholders to run through each of the options, filling in the tables as you go.

Let's take a look at an example. With the mathematical model example, we identified that the modeler wants to generate several output reports from the model. Now, if you are working in an iterative fashion with a development team (which you should be!) you will already be in discussion with them regarding the requirements. It may be that there are several options for delivering a reporting solution:

1. A reporting tool can be purchased 'off the shelf' and connected to the mathematical model
2. The development team can build their own reporting tool for the mathematical model.
3. The modelers can generate simple reports using software that they already have available, for example by copying and pasting information from the model into a standard presentation tool and then generating the report manually
4. Do nothing – do not provide the modelers with a reporting tool

Option 4, the 'do nothing' option, should always be included in any analysis.

So, how do we go about filling in the tables? Firstly, you need to create a SWOT analysis table for each option. Next, start with option 1 and think about the strengths associated with this option. What are the advantages of purchasing a reporting tool 'off the shelf'? Well, there would be no need to spend time developing something if a solution could be purchased. The users could probably get it straight away; no need to wait for something to be developed. It might be a cheaper option to buy a ready-made tool. And so on. Some of these strengths may prompt thoughts on opportunities. The users should be very helpful in suggesting potential opportunities. In this example, if they buy a tool and start using it, one potential opportunity might be that if they are able to generate the reports they need before the field trial season ends, they can plan in extra work and obtain more input from the additional evaluations.

When thinking about weaknesses, cost usually appears if the option is likely to be expensive. Time taken to configure the tool, maintenance costs, reliance on an external vendor for support… these could all be potential weaknesses. As for the threats, again the stakeholders will be better placed to provide some input, but generally the threats will probably be related to the weaknesses. One threat might be that the tool may not be easy to use, lots of configuration might be needed which would bump up the cost, maybe some customization of the tool will be required.

If we put all these thoughts into a SWOT analysis matrix, it might look something like this:

Fig. 59 – Example SWOT analysis for option 1 – purchase new reporting tool:

Strengths:	Weaknesses:
• No need to spend time developing a new solution • The users could use the new solution straight away • Cheaper than developing a new solution	• Maintenance costs • Time taken to configure the tool • Reliance on an external vendor for support
Opportunities:	Threats:
• If reports can be generated before the field trial season ends, extra work can be planned and more input obtained from additional evaluations	• Tool may not be easy to use • Lots of configuration might be needed which could increase cost • Some customization of the tool might be required

Now you would need to fill out a SWOT analysis matrix table for each of the other three options, but once you have this information documented you will be in a good position to discuss the options with the stakeholders and come to a consensual decision on what to do.

We have now come to the end of this (very) short chapter and in effect, the end of the book! Hopefully the information included in this book will enable you to use this approach on your own projects successfully, whatever development methodology is being used. And just to reiterate once again (and for the last time!), this approach is intended to provide you with a good foundation on which to build a solution… the building of the solution itself will probably require additional analysis work, including changes to or development of requirements. Good luck!

Appendix 1 – Some Useful Patterns

Pattern	Instructions
Create	1. Select to create object 2. Create using a template, a copy of a pre-existing object, or free form 3. Assemble components (record information) 4. Save (or don't save)
Change	1. Select to change object (edit / amend) 2. Make the change 3. Save the change (or don't save)
Add	1. Select to add 2. Add object 3. Save the change (or don't save)
Destroy	1. Select to destroy / remove (or archive) object 2. Make the change 3. Save the change (or don't save)
Search	1. Select to conduct search 2. Enter search parameters 3. Enter filter criteria 4. Run search 5. Save (or don't save) results of search
View	1. Select to view one or more objects / information (or view results of a search) 2. View the object(s) / information 3. Save (or don't save) the view
Review	1. Receive material for review 2. Carry out review 3. Record comments 4. Save (or don't save) comments
Track	1. Select to view status of object 2. View status of object
Send	1. Select object to send 2. Send object 3. Inform (notify) receiver that object is on its way 4. Change status of object to 'sent'
Receive	1. Select to receive (the object) 2. Receive object 3. Store object 4. Check object to ensure that it is valid
Import	1. Select to import 2. Select one or more objects to import 3. Select input location 4. Run the import
Export	1. Select to export 2. Select one or more objects (information) to export 3. Select output format 4. Run the export
Assign	1. Select to assign object to someone / something 2. Assign object 3. Receive confirmation that object has been assigned

For each pattern, think about the following considerations (in terms of functionality) that may need to be added to the instructions i.e. check through each of these with the stakeholders to determine of any are required or not:

a) Validation
b) Automated calculations or re-calculations
c) Mandatory vs. optional
d) 'Locking' of information (to prevent changes)
e) Use of 'look up' tables
f) Querying
g) Audit trail
h) Changing of status
i) Sending or receiving of notifications, acknowledgements or receipts
j) Automated prompts e.g. for initiation or confirmation of action
k) Visual displays e.g. highlighting, use of visual indicators etc.
l) Required attributes (recording, editing, searching or viewing)
m) Security considerations (access permissions)

Glossary of Terms

Term	Definition
Acceptance criteria	A set of conditions that need to be satisfied (and accepted) for a particular user story
Activity	A single step, operation or action that occurs as part of a workflow
Activity Diagram	A diagram used to describe workflows
Attribute	A quality or feature belonging to a concept (or entity)
Business Analysis	The set of tasks and techniques used to work as a liaison among stakeholders in order to understand the structure, policies, and operations of an organization, and to recommend solutions that enable the organization to achieve its goals
Business Concept	An object or thing or piece of information with a distinct and independent existence, something tangible that is used by a stakeholder within the business domain
Business Requirement	A high level requirement coming from the business i.e. 'the critical activities of an enterprise that must be performed to meet the organizational objectives while remaining solution independent'
Business Rule	A rule that defines or limits some aspect regarding the business. A business rule can apply to a business concept, a process or a step in the process.
Constraint	A limitation or restriction
Entity	A thing with a distinct and independent existence
Entity Relationship Diagram	A diagram describing inter-related things of interest within the knowledge domain
Functionality	The ability to do something with or to a 'thing'
Functional Requirement	A requirement that describes a single operation (or activity) that needs to be carried out in order to help meet a business requirement.
Mock-up	A model, used to enhance or generate understanding of something
Multiplicity	Multiplicity (or cardinality) states how many of one object can be associated with another object
Ontology	A semantic model that describes 'knowledge'
Problem Statement	A brief description of an issue that need to be addressed
Process	A sequence of inter-related steps or activities that begin with a triggering event and end with a result or outcome
Property	A quality or feature belonging to a concept (or entity)
Requirement	A need to do something with or to a 'thing'
Requirement Traceability	The ability to view the life of a requirement in terms of what is it associated with and where it came from
Root Cause	The actual cause of the problem / issue
Root Cause Analysis	Technique used to identify the underlying cause of the problem / issue
Semantic Data	The information that allows machines to understand the meaning of information (from Wikipedia)
Semantic Model	A data model which consists of a network of concepts and the

	relationships between those concepts
Semantic Web	The Semantic Web is an extension of the Web through standards defined by the World Wide Web Consortium (W3C). The standards promote common data formats and exchange protocols on the Web, most fundamentally the Resource Description Framework (RDF). (From Wikipedia).
SME	Subject Matter Expert
Stakeholder	A person, group or organization who has an interest in the problem / work area
Subject Matter Expert	Someone who has expert knowledge of the domain area
Swim lane	A diagrammatical artifact representing a 'role' e.g. 'phone user'
System Rule	A system rule defines or limits some aspect regarding the 'system'. System rules can often be associated with attributes
Traceability	The ability to verify the history, location, or application of an item by means of documented recorded identification
Trigger	An event that initiates (triggers) a process / activity step
Triple	A set of three entities that describe a statement about semantic data in the form of subject–predicate–object
Triple Store	A database containing triples
UML	Unified Modeling Language
Use Case	A sequence of actions that a user (or actor) performs to achieve a particular goal
User	Someone who is actually going to use the solution
User Story	A requirement that includes three elements: The 'role', the 'doing' part and the 'benefit', written from the perspective of a user
Workflow	A series of activities (operations or actions) that are necessary to complete a task

Bibliography

The following list of books are ones that I personally have found very useful and can strongly recommend:

Martin Fowler with Kendall Scott: *UML Distilled – Applying the Standard Object Modeling Language*

Doug Rosenberg with Kendall Scott: *Use Case Driven Object Modeling with UML, A Practical Approach*

Doug Rosenberg with Kendall Scott: *Applying Use Case Driven Object Modeling with UML*

Kendall Scott: *UML Explained*

Suzanne Robertson and James Robertson: *Mastering the Requirements Process*

Alec Sharp with Patrick McDermott: *Workflow Modeling – Tools for Process Improvement and Application Development*

Donald Gause and Gerald Weinberg: *Exploring Requirements – Quality before Design*

Debra Paul and Donald Yeates: *Business Analysis*

Dean Allemang and James Hendler: *Semantic Web for the Working Ontologist - Effective Modeling in RDFS and OWL*

Alistair Cockburn: *Writing Effective Use Cases*

Rebecca Wirfs-Brock: *The Art of Writing Use Cases*

International Institute of Business Analysts: *A Guide to the Business Analysis Body of Knowledge (BABOK Guide)*

Printed in Great Britain
by Amazon